Brilliant
BISCUITS

For Katherine and Eleanor.
"My favourite biscuits."

Acknowledgements
First thanks go to my partner, Paul, who has taken many, many biscuit photographs, helped out with designs, looked after our daughters and been a constant support. Thanks also to the two Sues, Cattermole and Paine, for all that childcare. Much appreciated.

To Wendy Butler, of the world-famous Wendy's Workshop, thanks for all your enthusiasm and encouragement. You are a great agent.

Thanks also to Caroline Smith, for all your wisdom and for being so gracious in the face of so many emails. To the rest of the foodie bunch out there, thanks for cheering me on.

And lastly, a big thank you to all those who have commissioned and enjoyed my biscuits. Suzanne, Louise, Natalie, Rocio, Mhairi, Liz, Susan, Lucinda and many others. I hope you and your families enjoy spotting 'your' biscuits.

Photography by Paul Cattermole and Pamela Giles

Brilliant
BISCUITS

Fun-to-decorate biscuits for all occasions

Pamela Giles

RIGHT WAY

Constable & Robinson Ltd
55–56 Russell Square
London WC1B 4HP
www.constablerobinson.com

First published by Right Way, an imprint of Constable & Robinson, 2012

A copy of the British Library Cataloguing in Publication Data is available from the British Library

ISBN: 978-0-7160-2322-7

Designed and typeset by Basement Press
Printed and bound in China
1 3 5 7 9 10 8 6 4 2

CONTENTS

BRILLIANT BISCUITS FOR CHILDREN

TROUBLESHOOTING AND SUPPLIERS

A WOMBAT ATE MY CUPCAKE

A lot of our cooking is about just getting a meal on the table. This can be satisfying for those who like to cook but the daily pressure to feed the family can erode any creativity or imagination that might have been part of the process.

Baking – and by that I mean the baking of the sweet treats kind – is different. Cakes and biscuits are non-essential to human survival, so they can be created purely for celebration, or eating pleasure. This gives the cook creative freedom. Something that is non-essential, nutrient-wise, is allowed to look pretty and be fun to make.

Biscuits as creative baking

The biscuits in this book are certainly that. They are baking that is enjoyable, satisfying and creative. Just as others like to sew, garden or make things for the home, I like to make and decorate biscuits for the creative outlet that they provide. The only difference is that biscuit decorating, as a creative hobby, is more likely to appeal to those who relish time in their kitchens, like me, rather than those who dread crossing the threshold.

I was already a keen baker before I headed down the biscuit road – my mother had me weighing out butter for cakes and sifting flour as a child. And I did dabble in the world of cakes and turn out some batches of cupcakes. But tasty as they were, they weren't quite as much fun. Biscuits are easy. Biscuits are fun. And biscuits are more imaginative. For me, anyway.

And so, when looking for an original, creative way of turning home baking into some income, rather than joining the army of cake bakers, biscuits were the answer for me. Not to dismiss the cupcake. I love the things, I really do. Especially lemon ones. I just prefer the originality, fun, colour and endless possibilities that biscuits provide. And so the title of this introduction reflects a bit of playful rivalry between baked goods. 'A wombat ate my cupcake.' Go wombat, go. Devour that cake.

Adventures in Biscuits

From the start, I knew that each biscuit commission that I took on would be a creative adventure. So 'Adventures in Biscuits' it was. That adventure quickly became lots of baking, decorating, photographing and general biscuit takeover of my kitchen.

Birthday parties are where the bulk of my biscuits go, though they really are for all occasions. Weddings, new babies, personalised thank yous, my kitchen has produced biscuits for them all. Part of the fun of offering a bespoke service to people is not knowing what will come next. Not too long after I created guide dog biscuits I decorated dinosaurs in full wedding kit. Seriously. I love these challenges.

Biscuit baking and decorating is very do-able. If you can work a rolling pin, you can do the rest. I am proof of that. Yes, I can bake, but I have never claimed to be able to do high-end cake decorating. Never a fancy wedding cake will my kitchen produce.

Simple decorating techniques

As for biscuits, my recipes are simple and the decorating techniques, after a few practice runs, are easy to master. Though if you are new to biscuiting – I am hoping the verb will catch on – you can work within your own creative comfort zone. Even just baking some basic shapes and decorating them with simple patterns for your own child's birthday can be immensely satisfying. And your children will be impressed.

To convince you, I have included a picture of the very first decorated biscuits I ever made. They were

for my daughter's flower-themed fourth birthday party. Bright colours (probably too bright), a serious overdose of glitter, masses of air bubbles and lots of wobbly lines. But she was thrilled (after reminding me that she

wanted only pink and no orange). The grown-ups present also oohed and aahed. Even now, two years later, I can remember how pleased I was with them, despite their obvious flaws. And I am still fond of them, enough to include their picture.

Don't make your biscuit baking and decorating about chasing perfection. Have fun with it and be proud of whatever you create.

Before starting out, you need to know some practical stuff first. Creating decorated biscuits is a three-step **design – bake – decorate** process, so you need to get a handle on how to come up with your own designs, the equipment you need, the recipes to use, how to mix up your icing and the basics of decorating. So please read through these sections before you decide which biscuit collection you want to tackle first. Take note also of the design, baking and decorating tips that are included within various biscuit collections. Each is there to provide a more in-depth explanation of a particular process or technique as it is relevant to that particular collection, but it can then be used elsewhere. A technique learned for one biscuit is easily applied to another. For reference, here is a list of these tips, and the pages where they can be found.

Design tips

Baking tips

Decorating tips

Cutters, colour and recipes

I have stated the cutters, colours and biscuit recipe that I used for each collection. I have kept the colour descriptions generic. 'Brown', for example, can be any brown made by any brand. I have only stipulated a particular shade when it is a particular one made by one brand. Wilton's 'Cornflower blue', for example, is a favourite shade of mine and appears more than once. The decorating steps are then specific to the biscuits shown on the pages. This is because some people, I know, like explicit instruction when they are new to a hobby. And I appreciate the inspiration that photos can provide. How often have we looked at something beautiful in a book or magazine and hoped that, when we make it, it turns out exactly like the photo?

This does not mean you should feel you have to replicate what I have done. I have emphasised the creativity that biscuiting allows, and encourage you to experiment. Change the colours, use different cutters, try out different techniques. If

what you try doesn't quite work, you will still have a biscuit to eat after you are done. The first point of departure from my designs should be with the glitter and sprinkles. Where I have used them, I have listed them as optional. Because they are, obviously. Just go with what you prefer.

The collections are ordered seasonally and thematically, representing a year of biscuit decorating. The year starts with Australia Day in January and ends with Christmas, but in between there are the various seasons and festivals, and all sorts of commissions. A busy year, but always fun. Happy biscuiting.

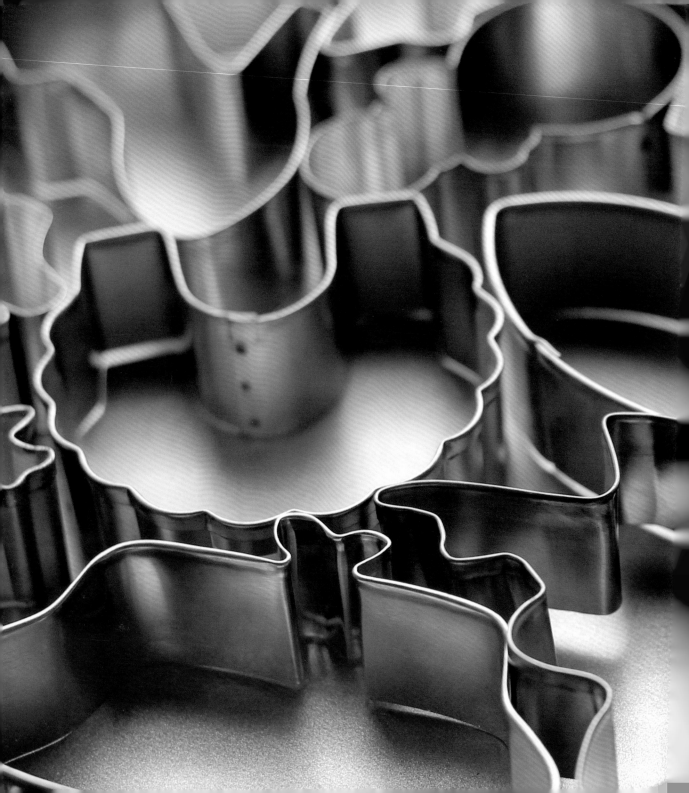

DESIGN

BISCUITS BY DESIGN

Anyone buying a baking book will no doubt peek at all the pictures first. It is, after all, seeing what you could, potentially, bake and create that inspires you to buy in the first place.

Plan before you ice

But, after looking at the pictures, any urgency you have to jump straight in and start decorating should be prefaced with a bit of planning. Every biscuit you see in this book was planned. Designed, even. No biscuit was 'made up' as I went along. Maybe this says something about my personality – I am the type of person who likes making lists – but I can't get started baking and decorating until I have a clear idea as to what I want the finished biscuits to look like.

And while the bulk of this book explains how to decorate specific biscuit collections, I hope that you will also feel sufficiently confident to create your own designs. Biscuit decorating should be more than colour by numbers. It is a creative process. For me, the planning is the best part as it is here that all the thinking is done – about colours, patterns, and so on.

Change the shape

Start your design planning by looking at your cutter. Don't assume that the shape you are given is the shape you are stuck with. Tinplate cutters are pliable, so can be squished and stretched a little. Helpful when, for example, I was faced with having a tortoise with a very flat shell. A quick bend of the cutter was all that was needed. And remember that the shape of the biscuit can also be adapted when cutting out your dough. If you don't like part of the cutter, trim it off the cut-out biscuit before baking. My cupcake cutter, for example, has a candle sticking out the top of it. I don't like this, so simply cut it off the unbaked biscuits.

Get sketching

The simplest and best way to figure out a design is to draw around the cutter onto some paper a couple of times and get sketching. As the cutter only gives you an outside shape, you need to have a clear

idea where lines and patterns start and finish on the biscuit. Animals are a good example. You need to sketch where lines for legs go, for starters. Look at the crocodile example shown here. When I used this cutter for the first time it was tricky to interpret. The shape just didn't make sense. Luckily, I have a husband who is good at interpreting these shapes. He sketched out all the curves in the tail and where the legs should go.

Sketching designs is also useful even when the shape seems obvious. Here are sketches for the 'Dad's toolkit' collection in this book. For these, it was important to sketch where handles started and finished, and to write down colour combinations.

If I can't make sense of a cutter I often pass it over to my husband's draughtsman's hands but when it involoves colour, I rely on my instincts. However, I have, more than once, raided my daughter's felt tip collection for a bit of therapeutic colouring in of a sketch. Even simply getting out all the food colours and lining up the contenders next to each other to see what looks good is helpful.

A design portfolio

Lastly, keep your designs as you may want to use them again. I keep mine in a clean, plastic folder.

BAKE

EQUIPMENT FOR BAKING

I always smile when reading those cookbooks that have as their subject the basics of cooking. They are often useful in telling you how long to cook a roast in the oven, but not so helpful when it comes to listing essential kitchen equipment. Many cookery writers will emphatically state that one needs only a minimal amount of kitchen tools and gadgets, and then go on to compile an extensive, and expensive, list of state-of-the art equipment deemed essential for cooking success. I always wonder what needs to come first, the significant cash outlay to acquire it all, or the extension to the kitchen to store it all.

Biscuit baking and decorating requires very little equipment. I say this honestly. While many readers at this point might be understandably thinking "But what about all the cutters?", the truth is that you do not need to buy dozens of the things in order to get going. A few basic shapes, such as a heart and a set of circles, lend themselves to all sorts of designs. So, here is my list of basic essentials, and my justification for their inclusion on such a list. For suggestions on where to buy, see Suppliers, page 189.

The essentials

Biscuit cutters

You don't need to fill a tea chest with them, but the reality is that if you have bought this book, you probably have a few lurking around a drawer somewhere anyway. A gingerbread man, or a star perhaps. A set of basic circles will cut scones and pastry circles as well as biscuits, and so are a good investment in any case. A basic round biscuit can be decorated in so many ways – faces, flowers, dots, swirls and so on. A set of hearts is useful as they suit any pattern. Kitchen and homeware stores often sell grèat cutter sets. For minimal outlay you can pick up a selection of themed cutters – Christmas, Easter, sea life, jungle, and many others. The cost of these sets is often far less per cutter than buying individually.

After this, what you buy is up to you. If you get obsessive, you end up with a collection of more than 300 and no box big enough to store them in. That is me, guilty as charged. But I can honestly say that it doesn't feel like I have squandered large amounts of money acquiring them, because the collection has been built up over years. And one cutter, bought on its own, costs very little. So, they are not an expensive thing to collect, and the collection has become a justification in itself. If I am a collector, collecting for a collection, then aren't I supposed to keep adding to it? Besides, it could be handbags or designer shoes. More costly, and you don't get to eat the results.

Baking sheets or trays

Again, something you are likely to have already. If you only plan on occasional, small-scale decorating, then the baking sheet you already have will suffice. If you think you might want to bake more than a dozen biscuits at a time, then get yourself another one or two. You can buy extra-large cookie sheets, which are a vast flat surface able to hold a pile of biscuits. Just check your oven is wide enough to fit them. (You can no doubt tell that I didn't do this when I bought one.)

Rolling pin

For rolling out your biscuit dough, obviously. I got my wooden one from a charity shop many years ago, and it rolls beautifully.

Re-usable baking parchment

You can bake biscuits on baking paper, or greaseproof paper but, since discovering this stuff I haven't lined a tray or a cake tin with paper since. It makes it onto the 'essentials' list because, rather than being a little luxury for those that bake often, these sheets really are brilliant for everyday use. Buy a few rolls and cut them to fit your cake tins and line your baking trays. Even if

you give up on being a supermum that churns out beautiful homemade biscuits and cakes, use a sheet when you bake fish fingers and oven chips for a weekend trash tea for the kids. Nothing sticks to the sheets, you give them a quick dunk and a wipe with the washing up water to get them clean, and you dry them simply by putting them in the turned-off but still-warm oven after cooking and clean-up. Store them with the tins and trays they have been cut to fit.

A thin spatula, palette knife or fish slice

Use one of these to lift biscuits that have been cut out from your workbench onto baking trays. No doubt there is something suitable already hanging about in your drawer. The only essential characteristic is that it is very thin and has a certain degree of flexibility. This will allow you to get underneath the biscuit and lift it without any breakages or pushing it out of shape. I use a very thin plastic spatula.

Food mixer

It is up to you, and your budget, to decide where along the mixer spectrum you lie, that is, where 'desirable' stops and 'essential' begins. But you need something. Our grandmothers may have turned out wondrous cakes and biscuits with only a mixing bowl and wooden spoon, but I have no idea how. I am lucky enough to have a KitchenAid freestanding food mixer. It felt like it cost a bomb at the time I bought it, but it is in constant use and for more than just biscuits. I don't know anyone who owns one that doesn't love it. The same goes for Kenwood owners, and their equivalents. They are a fantastic investment. As an alternative, hand-held mixers, the type that you slot beater attachments into and hover over a bowl to use, can be bought cheaply and don't take up space in a cupboard or deep drawer.

The desirables

Nice biscuit tins

Plastic airtight containers store biscuits perfectly well. But a natural extension to the cutter collection has been a growing pile of tins. An inexpensive option is to buy discount supermarket seasonal tins of biscuits, eat up the contents, and keep the tins. But then, nice sets of tins that can be stored inside each other are lovely to own. They can also store cakes, muffins and all sorts of other goodies, if you are looking for an excuse to buy a set.

Wire cooling racks

These are the wire racks that you turn cakes out onto to cool. Biscuits are fine when left to cool on a baking tray, but if you want to put that baking tray back into use to bake more biscuits, then a wire rack or two is useful for storing biscuits

when they have cooled enough to handle. I also use mine to lay biscuits out on when I am decorating.

Rolling guides

You can buy sets of these which, when attached to the ends of your rolling pin, provide a guide to the thickness of your dough. You get to choose how thick or thin you would like your dough and roll it uniformly. You can also buy rolling pins with these guides as a set. I would recommend such equipment only if you were considering baking and decorating professionally, and you were concerned about achieving total consistency. As for me, I have rolled out so, so many batches of dough that I trust my eye. And I am also quite attached to my trusty old wooden rolling pin.

MIX, ROLL, CUT, BAKE AND STORE

Before you even get near an icing bag, you need biscuits – the canvas for your icing designs.

The baking part may not seem the most exciting part of creating decorated biscuits, but it is important, as this is what you will taste. Sure, the big appeal of your biscuits, to start with, will be their beautiful appearance, but they still have to taste delicious. While many, many people have made the comment "They look too good to eat" about my biscuits, eaten they inevitably are. Not only do you want a biscuit that is tasty, you need recipes that produce dough that is easy to mix, roll, cut, bake and store. All of the following recipes stand up to the challenge: dough that is easy to work with that bakes delicious biscuits. But before you start reaching for ingredients, read through the following points, as they apply to whichever recipe you choose – including your own – and will make the biscuit-making process stress-free.

Mix

- Do an ingredients check before you start – finding you have run out of something halfway through a recipe is extremely frustrating.
- Measure out ingredients using reliable scales. I wouldn't be without my electronic scales. Metric and imperial measurements are supplied for each recipe. Use whichever you prefer, though don't mix them up. Use only ounces, or only grams, as amounts never convert exactly. For tablespoon and teaspoon measures, use proper measuring spoons, not spoons from the cutlery drawer. Just so you know, a teaspoon is 5 ml and a tablespoon is 15 ml.
- Make sure your butter is soft. Either take it out of the fridge in the morning you want to bake, or microwave it for 30 seconds or so on a very low setting.
- All egg sizes are large, which generally comes in at about 60 grams (3 ounces).
- If you are not confident separating eggs, do it over a small bowl rather than over your mixer bowl. If the yolk breaks, you can just start again. Once separated, keep the egg white and freeze it, or use it for your royal icing.

- All recipes call for butter. Whether it is unsalted or salted is up to you. If making for children, I use unsalted butter. If making for adults, I use slightly salted butter, or add a pinch of salt when mixing in the egg yolk. You do what you prefer.

- I use my freestanding food mixer for mixing my dough, but a hand-held mixer with beater attachments will also work fine. Just go slowly after adding the flour, as it can be messy.

- Chill your dough in the fridge before using it. When it is freshly made, it will be too soft to use. Chilling it a little means it will be that bit stiffer, and the cut-out biscuits will keep their shape.

  Form your dough into one or two flattish round lumps, cling film them, and then put them in the fridge. About 20 minutes should see the dough firm up sufficiently, though you can leave it in the fridge for longer. If it is super-hard when you take it out, just leave it on the kitchen counter top until it is pliable enough to roll out.

- The chilling stage means you can make your dough well in advance of baking. The dough will be fine in the fridge for two to three days.

Roll

- Have your equipment ready: rolling pin, cutters, baking trays lined with reusable baking parchment (ideally) or baking paper, spatula or palette knife, flour for dusting.

- Preheat your oven at the point where you start rolling your dough. You want it up to temperature by the time the first batch of biscuits is ready to go in.

- Keep the second of your cling-filmed dough portions in the fridge while you roll out the first. If you have had your dough in the fridge for longer, say overnight, then take both portions out about 20 minutes before starting, to give them time to soften up a little.

- Sprinkle a small amount of flour over your kitchen work surface. Also flour your rolling pin. This will stop your dough sticking. Sprinkle a bit more flour if needed, as you go. Don't add too much, just enough to stop your dough sticking to either the work surface or rolling pin.

- Have a tiny pile of flour on one corner of your worktop, to dunk your cutters in, to stop sticking.

- Roll out your dough evenly. Aim for about a five-millimetre thickness, but don't get your ruler out. Bend down to the level of the work surface and have a look: you will be able to see any obvious too-thick or too-thin parts.

- In some baking books, you will see strict instructions not to flour your work surface and rolling pin, for the reason that the extra flour will toughen your biscuits. Instead, instruction is given to roll out the dough between cling film, which can then be peeled off, or between sheets of baking paper, which can be laid straight onto the baking tray.

  I agree that you want to minimise the extra flour that is added to your dough, but don't think enough can be added during the rolling process to make a real difference to the final taste. Plus, the amount of flour in biscuit recipes varies considerably. My recipes are not flour-heavy and no one has ever said that one was 'tough'.

  Lastly, I have tried rolling dough between cling film and baking paper many times: the cling film wrinkles, the baking paper slips around on the work surface and it is hard to

get the rolled surface flat and even. So I don't try any more. But by all means give it a go. You may just find it incredibly easy.

Cut

- Tessellate your cutters so that you are cutting biscuit shapes as closely together as possible, to get the maximum number of biscuits from one roll-out of the dough.
- Pull the dough from around the cut-out biscuit shapes, don't attempt to lift the biscuit up and out of the rolled dough.

  Once you have removed excess dough from around the biscuit, lift it up carefully using a thin and flexible plastic spatula, or an old fashioned palette knife, and place it on your lined baking tray.
- Push together your scraps of rolled dough, so you can use them again. If the dough has softened too much, it will need another short stint in the fridge.
- Don't re-roll too many times. I don't go beyond two rollings. Too much handling can make your dough tough.
- If you are working in warm weather, or your

dough is starting to soften, place the baking tray in the fridge for 20 minutes or so to firm up the biscuits before baking.

If you are making gingerbread biscuits, don't skip the refrigeration stage at all. Gingerbread dough softens quickly and the biscuits are more likely to spread than with other recipes.

Bake

- Lay your biscuits close together on the tray so you can fit lots on, but leave about one centimetre between each. Make sure they are not touching.
- Keep biscuits of roughly even proportions on the same tray. If you mix up big and small biscuits, the smaller ones will finish baking before the larger biscuits. A little size variation is okay, just put the smaller biscuits in the middle of the tray and the larger ones at the edge.
- Bake in the centre of the oven. For best results, bake one tray at a time. Keep in the fridge any trays that are waiting for a turn in the oven.
- All ovens will vary slightly. This is why a range of cooking times is given for each recipe. Practising a recipe a few times will give you the confidence to pinpoint a more accurate cooking time.
- Don't just rely on the timer, use your eye as well. Once a biscuit is starting to show tinges of colour at the edges, it is done. This goes for all the recipes, including the chocolate one. You may have to look a little harder, but a slight darkening of the edges is what you are looking for.
- Don't be afraid to vary the cooking time depending on the biscuit size, or thickness. Smaller, thinner biscuits will obviously need less baking time than larger, thicker biscuits. If

- Store in an airtight container or tin. Put layers of kitchen towel or baking paper between the layers to separate them.
- Put the most fragile shapes on the bottom of your container, to minimise any breakages.
- Your biscuits will be fine stored in their container for two to three weeks, so you can bake well in advance of

you are baking smaller biscuits, it just makes sense to start checking a few minutes earlier.

- After taking the tray from the oven, leave it until it is cool enough to handle the baking paper or reusable parchment. Then, lift the whole sheet carefully by the corners and move to a wire cooling rack. Or, wait until the biscuits are cool enough to handle before carefully moving them one by one to the cooling rack, using a spatula.

Store

- Make sure your biscuits are completely cool before you decorate them. As decorating is time-consuming, I don't think I have ever managed to bake as well as decorate in the same day. Most often, you will need to store your biscuits overnight or for a couple of days before the decorating begins.

decorating. But bear in mind who is to receive your biscuits. If I am baking for a customer, I always decorate the biscuits as soon as possible after baking. While I know that biscuits, decorated or not, keep very well, it is always nice to be able to say to the person receiving them that they are freshly baked and decorated.

- You can freeze biscuit dough for up to three months, first making sure it is well-wrapped in cling film or a sealed freezer bag. Use straight away after thawing in the fridge. You can also freeze unbaked biscuits on trays, though I don't generally do this. If I have got to the stage where the biscuits are all rolled out, then baking them doesn't add too much more time to the process, no matter how late at night it is.
- Baked biscuits can also be frozen for four to six weeks. Make sure they are well wrapped in single layers, and thaw them at room temperature.

They also have blunter cutting edges as well, which are safer for little fingers. The disadvantage here is that it is more difficult to get a sharper, neater cut biscuit edge than with a metal cutter.

Plastic cutters won't rust but over time the plastic does deteriorate and the cutters can become brittle.

Copper cutters

These are the most expensive, and most decorative, of all cutters. They are generally handmade, and the shapes can be beautiful. Even second hand, they are collectible.

Copper is strong and sturdy, and will not rust. With care, a copper cutter can last a lifetime.

Over time, copper can tarnish. This does not matter, but if you want to restore its brightness, give it a swish in warm water with a small amount of vinegar or lemon juice added, followed by a polish with a soft cloth. Or simply buy a commercial copper cleaner.

Cutter care

For all types of cutter, the simplest way to care for them is to wash them as you would your other dishes. Wash them in the sink, with warm water and washing up liquid before rinsing.

Plastic cutters will be fine left to dry on the draining rack.

With metal cutters, I like to dry them quickly. Leaving them to air dry risks rust, in the case of tin cutters, and can also leave watermarks and detergent residue.

As I am often washing up after a biscuit-baking session, I give the cutters a quick dry with a tea towel, then place them in the turned off, but still warm, oven to dry them completely.

DECORATE

EQUIPMENT FOR DECORATING

You would be forgiven for thinking that you might need a pile of specialist bits and pieces in order to produce beautiful iced designs. Okay, there may be a couple of purchases to make, but they are minimal and, in the case of food colours, excellent value for money. Most will be, again, what you already have in your kitchen. How much additional equipment you acquire will depend on how often you find yourself baking and decorating. The more you do, the easier it is to justify buying new materials, and moving things from the 'desirables' list onto the 'essentials' list.

The essentials

Food gels or pastes

You can buy liquid food colours at most supermarkets and the colour range has expanded from the basic primary and secondary colours that were found in my mother's kitchen. The problem with liquid food colours, however, is that the colour range still isn't particularly vast, and I also believe they offer you a false economy. You usually need to use a lot of liquid to get a very strong colour so you could end up buying new bottles quite often. Using a lot of liquid also means you risk changing the consistency of your icing, making it too runny.

Gels or pastes are what you need. Yes, they are more expensive than the little liquid bottles. But as I have already suggested, the initial cost is rewarded by the longevity of your purchase, so making them a better investment. Because you don't need to use very much, your colours last a long time.

And yes, you have to be bothered to go to a specialist baking supplies shop, or order online, to get them, rather than dropping them into your supermarket trolley. This may be another disincentive to their purchase, but be reassured that you won't need to replenish for a very long time and, when you first use them, you will know you are using a superior product. Of all the 'essentials' that I list in this book, this is probably the most satisfying to buy. Lining up a selection of new little pots or bottles of bright, fun colours on your kitchen workbench is, for grown-ups who like to bake, the equivalent of the arty child being given a brand new paint set.

Icing bottles and nozzles

As the section on decorating basics explains (page 39), you need thicker (line) icing and thinner (flood) icing to decorate biscuits. To store your flood icing and to then use it to decorate, decorator's icing bottles are the most useful. They are available in kits and can also be bought individually (see Suppliers, page 189). They look similar to the squeezy vinegar and sauce bottles that you find in cafés and chip shops, and I am not all that convinced that these bottles wouldn't do the job perfectly well. All that is required is that the bottles dispense icing onto a biscuit in a regular flow.

For flood icing, I use number 4 nozzles. They have a plain round circle opening at the tip, so you can easily squeeze the flood icing out, but still control the pace and flow. These are readily available at baking supplies stores, or can be bought online.

which is all you need, easy to grip and control and are a lot cheaper than the disposable piping bags. So, when in this book I refer to 'icing bags' take that to mean the bag that you have chosen to use or happen to have in the house, be it freezer bag, sandwich bag (yes, I have tried them too) or disposable piping bag.

Small bowls or ramekins and plastic spoons

This may not seem like specialist decorating equipment, because it isn't, but it makes it onto this list because, if you are making up a selection of colours, you need lots of small bowls, ramekins or plastic tubs to mix them in, which not every household will have. I like to use lots of small ceramic ramekins, but you can simply recycle a few small deli pots with lids and you are there.

Why do I specify plastic spoons? Because when you are stirring food colours into small amounts of icing, that only require small bowls, ordinary teaspoons are too heavy and don't balance on the edge of your bowls or containers. This may all sound unnecessarily fussy, irrelevant even, but it is these little tips that can make kitchen projects that bit easier, and therefore more pleasurable. I use babies' plastic spoons. And the teaspoons that went with my daughters' plastic tea sets were, quite some time ago, quietly adopted by me. The girls haven't noticed, I promise.

Icing bags

For your thicker line icing you can, if you like, use the same icing bottles, but fit them with smaller nozzles (number 1 or 2). You can also use piping bags and fit them with the same nozzles. I dispensed with these nozzles a long time ago, the reason being that small nozzles block and clog all the time, which is annoying. A better option is to use disposable piping bags with the tips cut off to make a very small hole. (This is all described in more detail in the section on decorating basics, page 39.) These disposable piping bags can be bought at supermarkets, but if you run out, use small freezer bags. So long as they are flat ones where the bottom is not gusseted and the plastic is not too thin, they work fine. A friend who decorates biscuits passed this tip on to me and I have thanked her for it many times. If I am totally honest, I prefer them. They are small in size,

Cocktail sticks

The humble cocktail stick. Or, biscuit decorator's secret weapon. Sounds unlikely, but it is not far from the truth. The cocktail stick helps you to mix colours, unblock nozzles, straighten out blobs and wonky lines, create feather effects, and is a general all-round touch up and effects tool.

Wooden coffee stirrers

For quite a while, I searched for the ultimate flood icing spreader. I needed something that, once a load of flood icing had been squeezed onto a biscuit, could spread it right to the edges and into any corners. My big discovery was wooden coffee stirrers. They are perfect for the job as they are thin enough to direct the icing into small areas but still have a flat surface to smooth the icing. You can buy packs of them online.

The desirables

As with the section on baking essentials, what is desirable and what is essential is really a matter of opinion. The following can be helpful, but don't rush out to buy before you have done some actual decorating. I use these things from time to time; you may not want or need to.

Additional nozzles

Nozzles don't just come with round holes at the tips. You can get stars and flower shapes, among others. I rarely use them, but they can be used with very stiff royal icing to create decorative effects on biscuits. But I would only venture into this territory after mastering the basics of line and flood decorating.

Freestanding lamp

This may be up there with plastic spoons as being a strange inclusion on a list of equipment, but a freestanding lamp that you can set up at your table or workbench when decorating can be a real help, for the simple reason that you need to see clearly what you are doing. A strong light shining on to a freshly flooded biscuit will also show up air bubbles better (see Help, my biscuit has..., page 187).

Food colour pens

You can buy pens in a range of colours that you can draw straight onto biscuits, or dried royal icing. I have a black one that I have found useful to mark outlines or points on biscuits to guide line icing. Again, not essential but I quite like knowing that I have one to hand.

MAKING ROYAL ICING

My royal icing recipe

I have to confess that, before I wrote this book, I had never used a recipe to make royal icing. I simply placed three or four egg whites in the bowl of my food mixer, added a couple of tablespoons of meringue powder (not measured), then as much icing sugar as I thought I needed. Then, I mixed away, adding a bit of water if needed, to get the right consistency. I do appreciate, however, that this lack of empiricism could be off-putting, if not frightening, to those who have never made royal icing to decorate biscuits with. And so I got out my scales and created this 'proper' recipe.

Ingredients
900 g/2 lb icing sugar
4 egg whites
2 tblsp meringue powder
60 ml/2 fl oz water

- Put the icing sugar, egg whites and meringue powder into a very large bowl. Cover with a tea towel before mixing, otherwise your kitchen will be redecorated with icing sugar.
- Mix on a slow speed until combined. Add the water, trickle by trickle, until the right consistency is reached. You may not need all the water.
- To judge icing consistency, run a knife or plastic spatula through the surface of the icing and count.
- For line consistency icing (that is, the icing that is used to outline and make patterns on biscuits), the surface of the icing will smooth over after nine or 10 seconds. You want icing that is fairly stiff, but that doesn't completely keep its shape. Think toothpaste.
- For flood icing consistency (that is, the icing that is used to flood over the surface of the biscuit to cover it), the surface of the icing will smooth over after five or six seconds. You want icing that isn't runny, but has a gentle flow to it. Think custard that is thick, but still pourable.

Notes
- *The 900 g/2 lb of icing sugar stipulated here assumes you have bought a 1 kg box. As for the remaining 100g, use it to thicken coloured flood icing to create the thicker consistency required for line icing. For more details on this, see the section Mix, colour and store icing, page 35.*
- *This amount of icing should be sufficient to decorate 30–40 biscuits, depending on the size of the biscuits. The recipe is easily halved, if you need a smaller amount of icing.*
- *Many royal icing recipes contain only egg whites, or only meringue powder and water. I like to use both. Egg whites make your royal icing shiny and tough. Meringue powder, I believe, helps lock in the colour better, helping to prevent colour bleed. So use both ingredients to get the best results from your icing. I buy my meringue powder online, but you can get it in sachets from some supermarkets.*

Instant royal icing recipe

A great way to practise mixing to the right consistency is to use a packet of instant royal icing mix, where the sugar has meringue powder premixed into it.

Ingredients
900 g/2 lb instant royal icing
   sugar
180 ml/6 fl oz water

- Place the icing sugar and 150 ml/5 fl oz of the water in a very large bowl, cover and mix slowly. Add the remaining water, trickle by trickle, until you get the right consistency. You may not need all the water.

All meringue powder recipe

If you are decorating biscuits for sale, or know that the recipients might be uneasy about eating raw egg whites, consider using the instant royal icing recipe or, water and meringue powder.

Work on this ratio:

225 g/8 oz icing sugar :
1 tblsp meringue powder :
45 ml/3 tblsp/1 fl oz water.

Consistency: a reminder
When mixing up royal icing, whichever recipe you use, it is important to get the consistency right. This means you may need to add a touch more or less water than the amount stipulated. I like to mix to flood icing consistency (surface smoothes over after five or six seconds) and then add icing sugar after colouring to achieve line icing consistency (surface smoothes over after nine or 10 seconds). For more information, see the section Mix, colour and store icing, opposite.

MIX, COLOUR AND STORE ICING

Mixing up a big vat of royal icing can be very satisfying. The kitchen-coating properties of icing sugar clouds aside, once the mixing is done, what you have is a bowl of smooth, flowing, sweet icing. I love the way you can swirl a spatula through it, lift it up and watch the ribbons of icing fall back into the mass below.

Colouring the icing is even more fun, as it is at this point that all the design and colour ideas start to materialise. And of all the biscuit decorating steps, this seems to be the one that most fascinates children. My eldest daughter always wants to do the stirring: she thinks it is magical watching a tiny dot of gel paste transform boring white into a brilliant colour.

But before you begin creating your colour palette, read through the following, so you know exactly what to do when mixing, colouring and storing your icing. Along with stepping you through the processes, I have also included lots of tips to make it all quicker and easier and, hopefully, keep your kitchen that little bit cleaner.

Mix

- Make sure that, when you start mixing, your bowl is covered with a cloth. Icing sugar is so light and fine that the action of the beater or mixer attachment will send clouds of the stuff floating all over your kitchen.

- Remember to check the consistency of your royal icing carefully. I like to mix to flood icing consistency – the slightly runnier icing that you use to cover the base of a biscuit. After you have made royal icing a few times, you can trust your eye to tell you when it is just right. To be sure, count how long it takes for the surface to smooth over when a knife or spatula is dragged through the surface. A smooth surface after about five to six seconds is perfect.

- After mixing up your royal icing, get colouring quickly. It doesn't like hanging around, as the surface will start to dry out and form a crust, a bit like custard.

- Covering the bowl with cling film will stop the surface crust forming, but the cling film will collect a thick layer of icing when you peel it off. I prefer to keep the royal icing in its cloth-covered bowl, take out portions of it as needed, and just turn the food mixer on for 30 seconds here and there if it looks like the surface might start to harden.

- I often make a bit more royal icing than I think I will need. Before I start colouring, I scoop out about a cupful and put it in a sealed plastic container in the fridge. That way, if I find I run out of a colour before I have finished decorating, then I don't have to mix up another icing batch from scratch.

Colour

- Have all your equipment to hand. Icing bags and bottles, cocktail sticks, colours, spoons, bowls and so on. Count out how many colours you need and allocate a small bowl or ramekin, and a spoon, for each.

- Also keep a wet, wrung-out dish cloth on hand, or a packet of wet wipes. Royal icing is very sticky and you need something on hand to wipe up drips and spills as you go.

- Mix up one colour at a time. Don't pour out all the icing into the individual bowls and then start colouring. By the time you get to the last couple of bowls, the surface of the icing will have crusted over and you won't be able to use it. Just scoop out what you need for one colour, mix it up, and then scoop out another portion for your second colour.

- It can be tricky to judge how much of a particular colour you need. The way around this is to pour or scoop out a little bit more than you think you will need. Mix the colours that you know you will need the most of first. That way, if you are nearing the end of your icing supply but the only colour yet to mix is the one that you plan on using the least, then you will still probably have enough icing.

- If you are using bottles of food colour, you can invert the bottle and gently squeeze out a drop of colour. If the drop is heading into a small bowl of icing, unscrew the bottle cap and use a cocktail stick to dot a tiny amount into the icing. If you are using little pots of colour, using a cocktail stick in this way is the best method.

- Go slowly, and add a little colour at a time. For a lot of colours, you don't need to add much gel or paste to achieve a vibrant shade and, while it is easy to add more colour, trying to turn hot pink icing into baby pink, for example, is a bit more work. Remember that, when your icing dries, the colour will darken a little. So it is fine to colour your icing a touch lighter. Bear this in mind when trying to mix the three tricky colours: black, red and brown.

- Stir the colour into the icing thoroughly. This may sound obvious but, especially if you are colouring a large amount, it is easy to be left with white streaks if you don't scrape your spoon all the way around the bowl's sides and bottom to collect all the white icing.

- Once you are happy with your shade, pour your coloured icing – slowly – into your icing bottle, cap it and, if you are not decorating straight away, put it in the fridge (though a cold, unheated part of your house is also fine for a few hours).

- If you need line icing that is the same colour as the flood icing (which you most often do), leave three or four tablespoons of the icing behind in the bowl (depending on how many biscuits you need to decorate). Then add a teaspoon or so of icing sugar to the bowl, stir it in and check for consistency. For line icing, you are looking for the surface to smooth over after about nine or 10 seconds.

- As with flood icing, it can require a bit of guesswork when it comes to judging how much line icing is needed. I find that a good rule of thumb is to make more flood icing than you think you will need and less line icing. Quite a lot of flood icing can be required to cover a whole biscuit surface evenly but, with line icing, a little really does go a long way. If you want more reassurance, I have never run out of a line icing colour and rarely make up more than a few tablespoons worth.

- Spoon your line icing into your piping bag. If you are using the stiff disposable bags, this task can be made easier by standing the bag upright in a glass and folding the edges down. If you are using a nozzle with the piping bag, make sure you have put it in before spooning in the icing. Seal the bag by tying a knot in the end, use a hair tie, or use a plastic clip. If you are going for my budget alternative, the freezer bag, just flatten it out on the work surface and spoon your icing in. Squidge the icing down into one corner and then tie a knot in the bag to seal it. Keep your icing bags in the fridge until you are ready to decorate.

- While you are colouring your icing, spread a couple of squares of kitchen towel at the end of your work surface. You can deposit used wet wipes, cocktail sticks and any other detritus there as you go. Then, when you are finished, simply fold up the squares and bin them. This stops drips of colour getting on to your work surface which may need to be scrubbed off.

- When you have finished colouring your icing, wash up utensils and equipment that can't go in the dishwasher straight away. When dry, royal icing is very tough and it is a lot more effort to wash it off.

Store

- For best results, use your icing straight away. Having said that, it is fine to use it later the same day, or store it overnight.

- Keep all your mixed up icing colours in the fridge but take them out about 20 minutes or so before you want to use them, particularly if the weather is cold, so that the icing has a chance to come back to the right consistency.

- The longer your icing sits in the fridge without being used, the more it will start to separate. You will see little pools of colour forming as the water content of the egg white and food colour start to separate from the mix. To restore your icing, simply mix it again. For line icing, I simply pinch the open corner of the bag to block it, then massage the bag thoroughly so that the icing comes together again. For flood icing, I pour out the icing into a bowl, stir it thoroughly, then spoon or pour it into a new icing bottle.

- After a couple of days, you might want to think twice about whether or not you want to use your icing again at all. Let common sense guide you. If your royal icing contains unpasteurised liquid egg white, I would feel hesitant about keeping it for too long. If it is made with egg white powder, then I think it is safe to assume that it has a longer life.

- Think also about what the icing is to be used for when deciding how long to keep it for. If I am making biscuits for a paying customer, it is reasonable for them to expect fresh icing. Fortunately for me, a high biscuit turnover means constant batches of new icing. On the other hand, I have a habit of keeping leftover bags of line icing in a bowl in the fridge for up to a couple of weeks. This means that I can do some quick decorating on spare biscuits for friends and family using colours that I have to hand. This is great if I am trying out new designs or simply being nice mummy and creating some biscuit treats for my daughter's lunchbox.

- There isn't much point to keeping flood icing beyond a day or two. It separates quicker and a crust will form on the surface of the icing in the bottle.

- If you have icing leftover from a decorating project, but you don't have any more decorating on the horizon, then the decision is easy. There really is no point having it take up space in your fridge.

THE DECORATING BASICS

When people ask about how I go about decorating my biscuits, the initial questions are almost always about time, along the lines of, "How long does it take you to do all this?" It pleases me that people can glance at a decorated biscuit and instantly appreciate that a lot of time has been spent creating it. Because it has. Even a batch of simple biscuits with just a few icing colours can be an investment of many hours.

I understand completely if people don't want to try biscuit decorating for this reason. I often hear people say "I don't have the patience", or "I couldn't concentrate for that long." Fair enough.

But I wouldn't want anyone to be put off from giving it a go because they think it looks difficult. It isn't difficult. If it was, I wouldn't be doing it. Creating tiered celebration cakes with intricate decorations? Now, that looks difficult. But piping icing onto a flat biscuit isn't. Sure, first attempts don't produce the most professional results, but that is the case with just about any hobby. And some decorating techniques, such as icing intricate line details, are trickier than others, but that means simply not bothering with them until you feel confident enough to give them a go.

I am being totally honest in saying that there are only three things that you really have to get right to be able to master biscuit decorating.

1. Icing consistency. That is, having a 5–6-second smooth over time for flood icing and a 9–10-second smooth over time for line icing. This is

all covered in Making royal icing on page 33 and in Mix, colour and store icing on page 35.

2. Using line icing to create outlines and simple patterns.
3. Flooding.

Using line icing

Simply put, this means using the line icing that you have mixed up and spooned into icing bags, to create lines and patterns on your biscuits. You can outline a biscuit ready to flood it, or create any number of patterns and designs on the biscuit surface. Think of your line icing as felt tips for biscuits.

The snip

When you want to use your line icing, use very sharp scissors or a safety knife to snip a tiny hole straight across the tip of the bag. Make sure it is very small. It only needs to be big enough for the icing to flow out in a very thin stream. Check that the hole is the right size by squeezing the bag gently to check the flow and thickness of icing out of the bag.

Icing outlines or patterns

Hold the icing bag so that most of it is enclosed in your fist. This gives you better control over flow and direction. With the icing bag tip hovering just above the biscuit surface, squeeze very gently until you can see the icing emerge and touch the biscuit. At this point, gently lift the icing bag up and away from the biscuit, all the while maintaining the same pressure so that the icing continues to flow. Don't be tempted to squeeze a bit harder – the icing will flow too fast and you won't be able to control where it goes. With the icing bag held a good couple of centimetres above the biscuit, direct the bag, all the while watching the icing fall onto the biscuit. When you want to stop, quickly and decisively bring the tip of the icing bag down onto the biscuit surface, release pressure, and the line will stop.

Don't be tempted to keep the tip of the icing bag close to the biscuit surface, and to push the bag around the biscuit like a pen. It doesn't work, and you get wiggly, wonky, broken lines. At every decorating class I hold, people instinctively do this and need to be convinced to hold the icing bag up above the biscuit and let the icing fall onto it. They always work it out after a couple of

tries. I recommend practising first. If you don't want to sacrifice biscuits, practise on a baking sheet or on your kitchen worktop. Don't bother trying to create anything initially, just practise starting and stopping and icing a straight, unbroken line. Then, if you want to practise a design, draw it onto a piece of baking paper and then ice over the lines. This will give you the confidence to recreate your design on a biscuit.

Using flood icing

Outlining and flooding

If you want to create a biscuit that is completely covered with icing, it needs to be outlined and flooded. Outline the whole biscuit, or the section you want to flood, with line icing, and leave to dry.

I am often asked how long one has to wait for an outline to dry before flooding. I have never had to put a clock to work here – when making a big batch of biscuits, by the time the last one is outlined, the first is ready to flood. As a general rule, you are probably ready to go after about five minutes, with the longer the interval the more the outline will harden. Probably the best guide was provided by a fellow mum participating in a decorating class, who observed, "It is ready when it isn't shiny any more," meaning that the wet outline was shiny, but the dry outline was matt in appearance.

When the outline is dry, use your filled icing bottle to squeeze a generous amount of flood icing over the surface of the biscuit. Don't just blob a big amount in the middle, direct the nozzle or tip of the bottle around the area to be flooded. And don't think you are piling on too much, as you probably aren't. It takes a good amount of flood icing to get a thick, even coverage. You don't want to spread it too thin, as

then you won't get a nice, smooth surface when the icing dries.

After squeezing on the icing, use a wooden coffee stirrer, or lolly stick, or similar, to spread the icing into any corners and to smooth over any gaps.

When the flood icing is spread over the biscuit, give the biscuit a good shake. By this I mean gently holding it with your thumb and forefinger either side and giving it a good swish back and forth a few times across your table or work surface. You will see that any dents or divots in the surface of the flood icing will miraculously disappear, and the surface will be even and smooth.

At this point, scan over the surface of the biscuit for air bubbles. These are tiny bubbles of air that can be trapped in your icing. On a biscuit, as they attempt to rise upward through the icing, they can create a blip in the surface. If the air bubble makes it to the surface and pops, it can leave behind a little crater. Pop any air bubbles with a cocktail stick, then give the biscuit another quick shake on the work surface, then leave to dry.

Basic decorating techniques

Using line icing to fill

Your line icing can also be used to fill in small areas of a biscuit. Simply squeeze the icing gently out of the bag, then use the tip of the bag, or a cocktail stick, to push the icing where you want it to go. Or, outline with line icing, and then fill in the outline straight away. A duck's beak and patches on animals are all examples. You will see this technique referred to often in the decorating steps for many collections, and is expressed as 'outline and fill' rather than 'outline and flood'.

Adding patterns to wet icing

If, while your flood icing is wet, you add a second icing colour, then the second colour will settle into the flood icing and, as both colours dry, the biscuit's surface will be completely smooth. This technique works particularly well with spots. Simply invert your icing bottle and gently squeeze out a spot of icing, right onto the wet surface of the biscuit. When you are finished, give the biscuit another shake on the work surface to smooth out the icing.

Feathering and marbling

This technique couldn't be easier. To marble, after flooding a biscuit, add random blobs of flood icing, in a second colour. Then use a cocktail stick

to swirl through the icing surface, to create a marbled effect. For a feathered effect, ice lines of icing onto a flooded biscuit, when still wet. Drag through the lines with a cocktail stick, to 'feather' them, before leaving to dry.

Adding patterns to dry icing

For most biscuits in my collections, extra icing details are added after the flood icing has completely dried. There is no limit to what you can do. You can create animal eyes and other facial features, patterns on hearts and dresses, almost anything. In practically every case, line icing is used. The advantage of adding line details to dry flood icing is that the patterns dry in relief, really standing out from the flood base.

Drying decorated biscuits

For optimum results, it is best to leave flooded biscuits to dry overnight before adding finishing line details. Unless you live in a large house with no children, this may not be practical.

For this reason, I use my oven for biscuit storage when I have decorating projects on the go. As I finish a decorating stage on a biscuit, it joins others on a baking tray. When the tray is full, it goes back into the oven. I have even taking to buying baking trays with slightly raised edges, so that they can be stacked on top of each other at right angles.

The oven is turned off, but the fan is on. This helps the icing dry quickly. The obvious benefit of this is that, by speeding up the drying, I can get on with the decorating. The other big benefit is that faster drying helps keep the biscuits crisp. Leaving flooded biscuits to dry slowly can risk the biscuit base becoming soft, simply because the royal icing has a high liquid content.

If you don't have the option of turning on your oven's fan only, set the temperature to a very low 50º Celsius (120º Fahrenheit), with or without a fan. This gentle warmth will get your biscuits dry and keep them crisp. But don't leave it on overnight. Obtaining such a low temperature in a gas oven may not be possible.

Once you have finished decorating and drying your biscuits, store them in airtight tins or containers. I like to put kitchen towel between layers, as it seems to absorb any oiliness in the biscuits, which could otherwise leave marks on the iced surface.

A decorated biscuit will keep for up to three months. Seriously. Rarely do they last that long before being eaten, but it is a question people always ask.

COLLECTIONS

AUSTRALIANA

I have a special dispensation to make these biscuits. I am Australian. Even better, as Australia Day falls on January 26, it gave me an excuse to make them the first collection in the book. Celebrations of the day that the First Fleet landed in Australia in 1788 – that very first bunch of settlers – usually involve a barbecue, that most traditional, and stereotypical, Australian way of eating. Hence the photo. It really just had to be done.

The cutters
Kangaroo
Koala
Map of Australia
Wombat
If you have a suitably shaped pig cutter, it can be used for a wombat.

The biscuits
Vanilla with wholemeal

Icing – line
Red-brown
Made by adding orange or terracotta colour to brown icing.
Grey
Pink
Brown
Sand
Made by adding drops of yellow, orange and brown to white icing.
Navy blue
Red
Black
White

Icing – flood
Red-brown
Grey
Brown
Navy blue

Kangaroo
- Outline the main body of the kangaroo with red-brown line icing, leaving a small section for his white tummy. Flood with red-brown icing.
- When dry, use white line icing to fill in the tummy.
- When completely dry, outline the edge with red-brown line icing, adding curves to indicate front and back legs. When dry, ice small lines for claws, a dot for a nose, line detail inside the ears and a smile, using black line icing. Lastly, add an eye by placing a dot of black on top of a dot of white.

Koala
- Outline the koala's body with grey line icing, leaving a small section for his white tummy.
- Flood with grey. While the icing is still wet, place generous blobs of white line icing in his ears. With a cocktail stick, gently drag the white icing three or four times, to create fluffy fur. Leave to dry.
- Fill in the tummy section using white line icing.
- When the biscuit is completely dry, add an oval-shaped nose using black line icing.
- Outline around the koala's body with grey line icing, using curves to indicate the head, and front and back legs.
- When dry, add small claws, using black line icing. Add eyes by icing small dots of black on top of white and finish by icing a tiny line of pink under the nose, for a mouth.

VINTAGE TEA PARTY

If you are having a tea party, then biscuits are undoubtedly on the menu anyway. Here, the biscuits are the tea party. You may never, as a child, have sat down to an afternoon tea with delicate china teacups and pretty frosted cakes and lace doilies, but that doesn't matter. We can all visualise such an occasion as it might have happened in our childhood, and that is what I wanted to create with this collection: the romantic, nostalgic, afternoon tea. For mother's day, these biscuits would make the perfect gift.

The cutters
Teapot
Teacup
Dress
Cupcake

The biscuits
Basic butter biscuits

Icing – line
White
Aqua
Pale pink
Red

Icing – flood
White
Aqua
Pale pink

Icing – rosettes
Red
Avocado green
For how to mix icing for rosettes, see Decorating tip: Romantic rosettes.

Optional glitter and sprinkles
Glitter colours to match your icing colours
I used pastel pink and pastel blue on the dresses, and red for the cherries on the cupcakes.
A range of sprinkles and decorations to top your cupcakes.

Teapot

- I decorated the teapots and teacups in this collection both with aqua and white, and pink and white. Here I explain how to decorate in aqua and white but the steps are the same for both colour combinations.

- Outline the teapot in white line icing, remembering to outline a section to leave uniced, to indicate the handle. Flood with white icing and leave to dry.

- Create the red rosettes, arranging them logically on the teapot. I have followed a 2–1–2–1 pattern across the teapot. (See Decorating tip: Romantic rosettes, for how to do this.) Leave to dry.

- Outline the teapot with aqua line icing. Ice a small circle at the top and curved shape underneath for a lid. Put a lozenge shape at the bottom, for the base. Outline the handle and then put in the main lines around the outside of the pot. Add a little extra line across the spout. Then place small dots evenly between the rosettes, and evenly within the handle, top, base and spout.

- Finish off by icing two small avocado green lines around each rosette, for leaves.

Carefully add a bow, making sure your circles are big enough so that the icing lines do not run together to create a blob. While wet, sprinkle over blue glitter, if using, and leave to dry before shaking off the excess.

Cupcake

- For the cupcakes, I simply used the icing colours that I had mixed up for the teapots, teacups and dresses, along with a range of suitable sprinkles. Here are the steps for decorating a cupcake with aqua case and pink topping.

- Outline the cupcake case in white. Outline the two sides first, then ice four lines the same length as the sides down the cupcake base to the bottom. Make sure the lines are spaced evenly. Then create the ruffled top. Ice a small inverted 'v' at the top of each pair of lines. You should end up with five points. Then ice a line along the bottom of the case. Leave to dry.

- Flood each section of the cupcake case with aqua, using a cocktail stick to push icing into the corners. While the icing is still wet, add small white polka dots using line icing. Space them evenly. I

Teacup

- The steps for the teacups are similar to the teapot. First, outline with white and then flood. When outlining, remember to outline a small shape for the handle.

- Create the red rosettes. I did a cluster of three in the middle of the cup. Place the rosettes close together, but don't allow them to touch, so that each one is distinct and stands alone. Leave to dry.

- Outline the teacup with aqua line icing. Ice a wide oval shape at the top, then ice the cup shape. Then outline the handle and the saucer at the bottom.

- Finish by adding small dots. As with the teapot, follow a logical pattern and space your dots evenly.

- Finally, ice two small avocado green lines around each rosette, for leaves.

Tea dress

- Here are the steps for decorating a pink dress – the steps are the same for the aqua dresses.

- Outline the whole dress with pink line icing. When dry, flood with pink. While the icing is still wet, add polka dots, using white flood icing. Space them evenly. I started by icing two dots just underneath the bustline, and then spacing the dots from there. Do not place the dots too close the bottom edge of the dress, to leave space for the aqua trim. Leave to dry.

- Using aqua line icing, ice a wavy line along the bottom of the dress, two lines to trim the sleeves, and a line around the neckline. Add a straight line across the bust of the dress.

have followed a zig-zag pattern down each section of the case. Leave to dry.

- For the topping, outline in pink, then flood with pink. While the icing is still wet, press on sprinkles of your choice. If you are using larger sprinkles such as dragees or the sugar hearts shown here, don't just sprinkle or shake them on all at once. Place each one individually so that there is a space between each one.

- When the cupcake is completely dry, add a red cherry. With red line icing, ice a large red spot and then shake over some red glitter while it is still wet. Leave to dry before brushing off the excess.

DECORATING TIP: ROMANTIC ROSETTES

Little rosettes are easy to do, but very versatile. They are used here, but I have also used them to decorate Valentine's hearts and wedding biscuits.

The only thing you really have to get right if you want to create rosettes is the royal icing. It has to be super stiff. You only need small quantities. Here, I took some red line icing and added extra icing sugar to it. Keep stirring the icing sugar in until the icing doesn't smooth over. At all. You want it to be stiff enough so that, when you drag a cocktail stick through the surface or prick at the surface to make peaks, the icing keeps its shape.

For the green leaves, I took a small quantity of white line icing, added a tiny dot of avocado green colour, and then stirred in extra icing sugar in the same way as for the red.

To create the rosette, simply ice a very small, very tight swirl, building it up sufficiently so that the rosette has some height. Once you start, don't stop your icing swirl until you have reached the centre. Then lift away the bag, creating a small peak of icing in the middle to represent the centre of the rosette. It is exactly the same action as if you pick up a pen and draw a spot. You naturally draw a round shape and then keep moving the pen round and round until the spot is filled in. I recommend practising with a few rosettes on your work surface before decorating the actual biscuits.

When the rosettes are dry, add leaves, which are simply two small lines of green on either side of each rosette. Rotating the biscuit a few times while adding the leaves makes the overall effect more natural, with the leaves placed randomly rather than uniformly.

FOR THE FASHIONISTAS

Girls love their shoes. And bags. And pretty dresses. And here, in the 1920s flapper wardrobe, hats and fans as well. Here we have geometric art deco-inspired patterns, sequins, block colours and oodles of jazz age style. This is the collection for those who love all things vintage, classy and timeless.

The cutters

Fan
Shoe
Hat
Bags (clutch and shoulder)
Flapper dress
I used the same cutter that made the dresses in the 'Vintage tea party' collection, but cut off the sleeves and slimmed down the skirt.

The biscuits

Vanilla with wholemeal, or chocolate

Icing – line

Black
Peach
Ivory
Yellow

Icing – flood

Black
Peach
Ivory

Optional sprinkles and glitter

Sugar flowers
Black glitter
Ivory glitter
Gold glitter

Fan

- With ivory line icing, outline and fill a long section down the side of the biscuit, for the fan edge. When this is dry, repeat the pattern on the other side of the fan. Leave to dry.

- Outline the main body of the fan with peach line icing, flood with peach, then leave to dry. Leave a section of biscuit uniced at the top.

- With black line icing, outline and fill a small wedge shape at the bottom of the fan. Leave to dry completely.

- Add line detail and dots with black line icing. I put a scallop pattern along the top, and two scallop rows underneath this first row. I then added nine lines of dots, with the dots decreasing in size. If you like, add black glitter while the icing is still wet. Leave to dry, then shake off the excess.

Flapper dress

- Outline the whole biscuit with ivory line icing, flood with ivory, then leave to dry completely.

- Use ivory or black line icing to add patterning. I started by making a small diamond shape in the centre underneath the neckline, then radiated out four lines either side. I then added five rows of scallop patterning down the front of the dress, iced a series of vertical lines for the skirt, and finished with a curvy row along the hemline.

- If you like, add black or ivory glitter. If you are using glitter, try to work quite quickly, so that the icing does not dry. Rather than trying to target the glitter over the lines, cover the whole biscuit. Leave to dry, then shake off the excess.

Shoes

- **Peach shoe:** Outline the shoe with peach line icing, leaving the heel and toe sections bare. Flood with peach and leave to dry.

- Use black line icing to outline and fill the toe and heel. Give the biscuit a good shake, then leave to dry.

- Add black line detail. A line along the top length of the shoe, two curved arcs at the shoe's front and three curved arcs over the heel. Add black glitter, if you like.

- **Ivory and black shoe:** Outline the back section and the toe of the shoe with black line icing. For the toe, create a scallop edging. Flood with black and leave to dry.

- Outline the heel and middle section with ivory line icing, flood with ivory, then leave to dry completely.

- On the toe, use ivory line icing to create three long tear drop shapes, finishing with a point. Shape the icing with a cocktail stick, if needed.

- When dry, use black line icing to add three or four v-shaped patterns over the ivory section of the shoe. Add black glitter, if you like.

- **Black shoe:** Outline the main body of the shoe, leaving the toe, heel and a section along the top uniced. Flood with black and leave to dry.

- Outline the heel with black line icing, flood with black and leave to dry.

- With ivory line icing, outline and fill in the toe, and the section along the top of the shoe.

- When dry, use peach line icing to stick on a small sugar flower, if you like.

Hat

- Outline the whole biscuit with ivory or peach line icing, flood with the matching flood icing, then leave to dry completely.

- Use line icing to add a hat band. I used black on the peach hat, and peach on the ivory hat. Use a cocktail stick to smooth and shape the icing. Leave to dry.

- Use ivory line icing to add a pattern of dots at one end of the band. Add ivory glitter, if you like.

Clutch bag

- Outline the main section of the bag, with ivory or peach line icing. I put a small dot of icing at the point of the 'v' before starting out, to make sure the point was in the

centre. Flood with the matching icing and leave to dry completely.

- With black line icing, outline a wedge shape to fill the v-section, flood, then leave to dry.

- Use ivory line icing to outline the bag's handle, flood, then leave to dry.

- Add black line detail. A 'v' pattern on the black section, and vertical lines running down the main section of the bag. Ice the middle line first,

from the point of the 'v', then add an equal number of lines either side.

- Add black glitter, if you like.

Shoulder bags

- **Ivory bag:** Outline the square section of the bag with ivory line icing, flood, then leave to dry completely.

- Use ivory line icing to outline and fill a handle section. Shake the biscuit, then leave to dry.

- Use yellow icing to add a line across the top of the bag, and

a smaller line in the middle, for a clasp.

- For the patterning, add the black lines first. I laid a cocktail stick down the centre of the biscuit, to act as a guide. I then added lines on one side, then added the corresponding lines down the other side. Add black glitter, if you like.

- Use peach line icing to add lines either side of the black lines.

- **Black and peach bag:** Outline the square section of the bag

with black line icing, flood, then leave to dry completely.

- Use peach line icing to outline and fill square patterns on the black, then leave to dry.

- For the gold chain handle, use yellow line icing to create a pattern of dots all around the handle section. I trailed the dots, to suggest the chain's looseness. Also add a small line of yellow, for a clasp. Add gold glitter, if you like.

DECORATING TIP: **GETTING GLITTERY**

I am a bit of a sucker for edible glitter. The pots are tiny and expensive, but only a little of the stuff goes a long way. And the effect can be transformative. Your biscuits, beautiful already, become twinkly and sparkly, with very little extra work from you.

All you need to use is a fine tea strainer, piece of paper, soft paintbrush and a spoon. The latter needs to be very small to be able to scoop into the tiny pots. I use a very petite pink plastic one that came with a toy doll's accessory set.

When using glitter, it is important that the icing that you want the biscuit to stick to is very wet, and the rest of the icing on the biscuit completely dry. For this reason, add the glitter biscuit by biscuit, one at a time, as soon as you have added the icing that you want to add glitter to. It won't work to ice a few, and then glitter them all. By then, the icing will be too dry.

To use, simply place the biscuit on a piece of paper, hold a tea strainer close to the biscuit surface, spoon in some glitter, then gently shake away. Go for a thick coverage, for maximum glitter stickage.

When you are done, gently lift up the biscuit and, holding it by the edges, turn it over and give it a tap on the back. This will knock off most of the excess glitter. When the biscuit is completely dry, use a soft paintbrush to brush the rest of the biscuit clean, over the same piece of paper.

A useful tip here is to fold, then unfold, the piece of paper that you are glittering on. Then, when you are finished, the excess glitter that has been brushed off can easily be poured, down the fold, back into the pot.

I keep separate pieces of folded paper for different colours of glitter. I have simply written 'black', 'pink' and so on, on each sheet. This is because specks of the stuff are always left behind, and you don't want specks of black ending up in your pink pot, for example, the next time you use those colours.

Another tip is to keep a cocktail stick handy when glittering. If a stray speck of another colour ends up on your biscuit, simply use the cocktail stick to push it into the wet icing, to make it disappear.

I should add that while it is never compulsory and certainly, many biscuit designs do not call for any glitter, if you are making children's birthday party biscuits, do not hesitate. In my experience, children will always go for a glittery biscuit, if given the choice.

And lastly, glitter is great to call into service if your decorating isn't working out as well as you like. If your spots are a bit wobbly or your lines are a bit wonky, glitter them. People won't notice any of your mistakes, they will be dazzled instead by all the sparkle. This is why I like to call glitter 'makeup for biscuits'. It covers up any number of blemishes.

A VISIT FROM THE STORK

A new baby, another excuse for a biscuit collection. Why not? No, the baby won't get to eat them, but the no-doubt fretful parents, particularly if this is a first baby, will appreciate a biscuit treat. Plus, like many of the collections in this book, a new baby also has so much to offer the biscuit decorator when it comes to cutters and colours. Pastels, polka dots, cutesy shapes. All that remains is to coo adoringly.

The cutters
Babygro
Bib
Duck
Rattle
Building block
Pram
Bottle
Newborn

The biscuits
Vanilla with wholemeal

Icing – line
Cornflower blue
Ivory
Lemon yellow
Dark brown
Skintone
Made by adding drops of pink and brown to ivory, then lightening with white.
Black
White

Icing – flood
Cornflower blue
Ivory
Lemon yellow

Note on colours
These pale colours were mixed using white food colour (see Decorating tip: Mixing colours with white).
*   For a baby girl, just swap the blue for a pale pink, as I have shown in some examples here.*

Babygro
- Outline the biscuit with cornflower blue line icing, flood and leave to dry completely.
- Use ivory line icing to add three medium-sized dots along the bottom of the babygro, for poppers, and add curved lines along the neck, sleeve and leg edges.
- When dry, add two blue lines running from the neckline to the underarms, to indicate seams.
- Ice a series of straight lines up the front of the babygro, starting from the bottom and working upwards, using ivory line icing. Add more corresponding lines on the two sleeves.

Bib
- Outline the bib with cornflower blue line icing, leaving the frilled edge and a rectangular section in the centre, flood and leave to dry.
- Use ivory line icing to outline and fill the rectangular-shaped middle and the frilled

- Fill in the beak section with dark brown line icing.
- Add line detail to indicate the duck's wing and tail feathers. Finish with a dot of black on white, for an eye.

use too much, or the parts of the bow will run in to each other.
- Lastly, outline the handle section with blue line detail.

Building block

- Outline with lemon yellow line icing, flood and leave to dry completely.
- Use cornflower blue line icing to mark out the block faces. Then, use lemon yellow line icing to ice squares inside the blue lines.
- Finish by adding letters or numbers of your choice. I went for an 'R', for baby Reece's name, and the numbers represent his birthdate, February 12.

Pram

- These are the decorating steps for a baby boy's pram.
- Outline the main carriage section with lemon yellow line icing, flood and leave to dry completely.

edge. Shake to smooth over and leave to dry.

- With blue line icing, add a pattern of very small dots on the bib. With ivory line icing, outline the frill section, so that it stands out.
- Add line details on the middle section, in blue. I iced this baby's birthdate along with small lines around the edge, to look like stitching. Names or initials would also be a good choice.

Rattle

- With lemon yellow line icing, outline a ring-shape on the handle. Fill with the same icing.
- Use the same lemon yellow to outline the large round section, flood and leave to dry.
- With cornflower blue line icing, outline two blue sections over the top of the yellow circle, then flood with blue and leave to dry.
- Use skintone line icing to fill in the rattle stem. When dry, use blue line icing to create a bow. Ice an outline first, then fill with the same icing. Do not

Duck

- Outline the duck with lemon yellow line icing, leaving a section for the beak, flood and leave to dry.

Newborn

- Outline the kerchief section with cornflower blue or pink line icing, and flood. While the icing is still wet, add dots of ivory flood icing. Leave to dry.
- When dry, outline and fill the baby's head and leg with skintone icing. Leave to dry completely.
- Finish by adding face detail: a tiny curl of dark brown hair, a dot of black on white for an eye, a tiny skintone curve for an ear, and an even tinier dot for a nose.

- Outline the hood section with cornflower blue line icing, flood and leave to dry.
- On the carriage body, use blue line icing to outline and fill a heart, then leave to dry.
- Use dark brown line icing to mark out wheel spokes. When dry, dot the centres with lemon yellow and, while you have the icing bag in your hand, add dots down the front of the hood.
- Add blue line detail to the hood: ice the curved outline first, then add the four straight lines.
- Finish by adding lemon yellow line details: an outline around the carriage body with a scallop-edge top, dots around the edge of the heart and a letter of your choice in the heart's centre.

Bottle

- Outline the main bottle section and teat at the top, with ivory line icing, flood and leave to dry.
- Outline the cap section with cornflower blue line icing, flood and leave to dry.
- Finish the bottle with blue line details. Outline the cap section again, and add about six or seven vertical lines down the cap. Add alternate short and long horizontal line markings down the body of the bottle, to indicate volume.

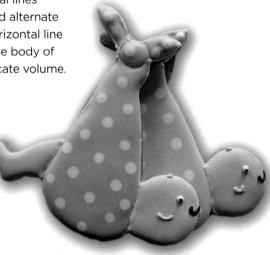

DECORATING TIP: **MIXING COLOURS WITH WHITE**

It may sound strange for me to say that white is the food colour I go through the most of when, after all, icing starts out white.

But let me elaborate on the many uses of white. First, it makes your white icing properly, starkly, brilliantly white.

But I can't stop there when writing about white. I also use it all the time to lighten colours if I have added a touch too much gel or paste, or simply want a lighter shade. If I am attempting to create my own icing shade by mixing colours, white is inevitably used at some point. Mixing to create the skintone colour used here is a good example. I added tiny drops of pink, brown and ivory, then lightened up the whole mix with white (remembering that the colour would darken a little when drying).

For this collection, I purposefully added white to all the colours that I mixed. I could have just used a tiny amount of yellow, blue and ivory colour to the icing to create the pale shades I was after but, have a closer look at the colours on these biscuits – the colours are pastelly and pale, but still strong, solid and matt in finish. This is the white colour at work.

I am not totally sure why, and I discovered it purely by chance, but if you are only adding a tiny amount of another colour to your icing, particularly a bright colour, add white as well. The white takes the bright sting out of your colours, turning your icing into a cohesive, creamy, matt emulsion. Think of it as moving from children's felt tips to a Dulux colour chart.

SPRINGTIME SONGBIRDS

The arrival of spring seems to be given such brief attention, being quickly overrun by Easter and its team of rabbits and chicks. But what I really like after all the long winter months is hearing birdsong again in the morning, as the sunshine dares to appear that bit earlier. These birdies – sweet, folksy, altogether charming – are my way of marking the change of season.

The cutter
Birdie
This design is adaptable to any simple, classic bird shape. Note also that some birds are perching, with feet, and some are flying, with no feet. For the flying birds I simply cut the feet parts off when cutting out the biscuits.

The biscuits
Chocolate and vanilla with wholemeal

Icing – line and flood
Cornflower blue
White

The songbirds

- First, I divided up my batch of biscuits. I then outlined in blue or white and, when dry, flooded with the matching colour and left to dry completely.

- The patterns on the songbirds are easier to recreate than they may look at first glance. I created mine by using simple dots, scallop patterning, lines and teardrop shapes. You can use almost any combination of these that you like, as well as some of your own ideas. Hearts and little daisy-like flowers would work.

- Sketch out your ideas first to get an idea of what the finished biscuit will look like. I sketched out six designs, and then picked the best four.

- For the white perching birds, I added the tail decoration first, followed by the wing outline. I then added the eye, feet and beak, before adding the line patterns in the wing.

- For the blue flying birds, I added the beak, eye and tail decoration first, before concentrating on the patterning on the bird's underbelly.

- For some of the birds, there are tiny white dots on blue line icing, and tiny blue dots on white line icing. To do this, I waited until I had finished decorating the entire batch of biscuits, then simply added the extra dots where they were needed.

- Another thing that makes these designs quite easy to recreate is the humble cocktail stick. Instead of attempting to ice the exact shape of the beak, for example, I iced an approximate shape, and then used a cocktail stick to push and drag the icing to create the pattern or shape I wanted.

EASTER EGGSTRAVAGANZA

Decorating Easter egg biscuits presents you with limitless options. Just think of all the colours and patterns to be found on the foil wrapping of chocolate eggs, for starters. And I would certainly recommend using these for inspiration. When I made this collection, the egg cutter I used was really big, 10 cm tall. So I wanted a big, bold design. I flipped through a book I had on Fabergé, but couldn't get paisley out of my head, along with an unexplained desire to use bright pink and green. As for the end result, I like to think that if Carl Fabergé had been fashioning his wonderful bejewelled eggs in the 1970s, they might look a little like these.

The cutter
Egg

The biscuits
Chocolate and vanilla with wholemeal

Icing – line
Ivory
Fuschia
Pale pink
Leaf green
Pale green

Icing – flood
Ivory
Pale pink
Pale green

The eggs
- First, I divided my batch of biscuits into three, and then outlined in pale green, pale pink or ivory line icing, before flooding with the same colour and leaving to dry.
- I then decorated the eggs with three variations of my paisley design, and give steps for three examples.

Green paisley egg
- Using pale pink line icing, ice the basic shapes for the paisley droplets. Ice one big droplet coming in from the left, and two smaller curves at the top and bottom right, to make part-droplets. Note that, as you are icing these shapes freehand, not every droplet, or part-droplet, will be exactly the same size and shape. This does not matter, but make sure you err on the side of making the droplets smaller rather than larger, leaving space between them so they do not touch, and room for the smaller icing patterns.
- Using the same pale pink line icing, ice the two very small droplets, one at the top and one at the bottom of the egg.
- When dry, add droplets inside the pale pink droplets, using ivory line icing. Make sure

there is a decent-sized gap between the line of pink and line of ivory, so you have space for the rest of the patterning. Ice spots inside the droplets using ivory line icing. Fill in the two very small pink droplets with ivory line icing.

- Using pale pink line icing, carefully ice a scallop edge along the inside of the big pink droplets. Try to keep this patterning small. Leave to dry.

- Using leaf green, ice a line of small dots in the space left between the scalloped edge and the ivory droplets. Then ice another series of dots around the edge of each droplet, large and small, using fuchsia line icing.

- To create the patterning between the droplets, simply ice a lot of small dots, using pale green line icing. Do not put the dots too close together. Also add three or four dots of pale pink line icing, to turn into mini flowers. When the pink dots are dry, place four larger dots around them, using pale green line icing. When dry, put small dots of ivory line icing between each green petal.

Ivory paisley egg

- Using leaf green line icing, ice the basic shapes for the paisley droplets. Place one large droplet on the left of the egg, a much smaller one on the bottom right, and two small tails: one at the bottom left, and one near the top right.

- When dry, add pink droplets inside the green droplets. For the large droplet, outline the inner droplet with pale pink line icing and then fill with the same icing, giving the biscuit a good shake to smooth the surface. For the smaller droplet and droplet tails, simply ice a very small section of pink in the middle of each. Make sure there is a gap between the line of green and the inner pink droplet.

- Using leaf green line icing, ice a scallop pattern inside the green droplets, keeping it small. Leave to dry.

- Using pale green, ice lines of small dots between the scallop pattern and the pink droplets. Then ice a series of fuchsia dots around the outer edge of all the droplets, using fuchsia line icing.

- To create the patterning between the droplets, simply ice a lot of small dots, using ivory line icing, but not too close together. Also ice three pale pink dots, to turn into mini flowers. When the pink dots are dry, place four larger dots around them, using ivory line icing. When dry, put small dots of pale green line icing between each ivory petal.

Pink paisley egg

- Using pale green line icing, ice the basic shapes for the paisley droplets. For this egg, they are mostly part-droplets: one with its tail missing extending down across the egg from the right, one complete droplet occupying the space at the top of the egg, one small curve at the top left, a tail at the bottom left and a curved droplet part along the bottom right.

DESIGN TIP: IT'S ALL IN THE RESEARCH

For a lot of biscuits the design is, largely, suggested by the shape of the cutter. I usually decorate animal biscuits, for instance, as the cutter suggests the animal should look.

With basic shapes such as the eggs here, hearts, circles and stars you have a lot more freedom. Really, anything goes. And this is where you get to carry out your design research. While you may have ideas already in your head, look to other sources as well. Homewares catalogues, wallpaper, wrapping paper, greetings cards and patterns on things around your home, such as crockery, can all be starting points for your design and give you colour ideas.

With my eggs, I started by browsing a book pulled from the bookcase about Fabergé eggs but kept coming back to paisley. A quick bit of Googling produced a pile of paisley images. I picked one I liked and printed it off. I then laid the egg cutter over the printed page and moved it around, looking for the right, balanced compositions. (My high school art teacher would have to be impressed at this point.) When I had selected the sections of the print-out that I wanted to use, I traced around the cutter shape and then adapted the pattern within to come up with an icing-friendly design.

By icing-friendly, I mean a design that was far simpler than the printed pattern, and able to be iced onto the biscuits. I kept the basic droplet shapes and scalloped edges but made the inner droplets a simple, solid colour instead of having detailed patterning within them. I also opted for a simple patterning between the droplets: dots and mini flowers.

- When dry, add leaf green droplets within the pale green droplets, using line icing. Fill with the same icing.

- Using pale green line icing, ice a scallop edge along the inside of each part-droplet and leave to dry. Then outline each leaf green inner droplet with dots, using ivory line icing.

- Around the outside of each light green droplet, add lines of fuchsia dots, using line icing. Leave to dry.

- For the background patterning, ice a lot of small pale pink dots, along with three or four larger dots, to turn into mini flowers. When the pink dots are dry, place four larger dots around them, using pale pink line icing. When dry, put small dots of leaf green line icing between each pink petal.

THE SECRET GARDEN

This is a very special garden, designed without neatly edged borders and immaculate lawns but to represent the type of garden that inhabits little girls' imaginations: one filled with bright flowers, jewelled dragonflies and smiling ladybirds. This is the garden where the bumblebees are always busy, the butterflies land on your shoulder and adults are nowhere to be seen.

The cutters
Daisy
Butterfly
Dragonfly
Snail
Caterpillar
Ladybird
There are many different flower and butterfly cutters available, and yours may differ from mine. Just adapt the designs to fit.

The biscuits
Vanilla with wholemeal

Icing – line
A selection of bright colours
I used green, purple, pink, yellow, aqua and blue.
Red
White
Black

Icing – flood
Flood icing to match your chosen bright line icing colours
Red
Black

Optional glitter
Glitter colours of your choice
I used pastel lilac, pastel pink, pastel lemon and jewel ocean spray.
I have only instructed to leave the glitter to dry before brushing off the excess, in the first instance, but this process is carried out whenever glitter is applied.

Purple and blue butterfly
- Outline and flood the whole biscuit, using purple icing, and leave to dry completely.
- With blue line icing, add a curved line all the way down each wing, starting with a curve at the top and finishing with a curve at the bottom. Straight away, add two small lines, to make a v-pattern extending out from the mid-point of the curved line. If using, add lilac glitter straight away.
- Use pink line icing to add four dots down the middle of the butterfly, and to fill in the triangle sections at the top

and bottom. Shape with a cocktail stick, if needed.
- Use the same pink to add dots to the bottom tips of the wings, and the outer top tips of the wings. While still wet, top these dots with blue line icing.
- Add matching sets of three dots around the curves of the wing sections, and on either side of the pink and blue dots at the wing tips, using pink, yellow and blue line icing.

Purple and pink butterfly
- Outline the whole biscuit with purple line icing, then flood with purple and leave to dry.
- Ice an oval-shaped section down the middle of the butterfly, for its body, using pink line icing. Then, with the same icing, outline around the outside of the wings. On each wing, continue the line in toward the middle of the

biscuit and finish the line with a medium-sized dot. If you are using pink glitter, add it straight away while the icing is still wet. Leave the glitter to dry before brushing off the excess.

- Using aqua line icing, add six or seven dots down the middle of the body, for segments. Use a cocktail stick, if needed, to drag the icing to fill the point at the bottom. With the same aqua, add medium-sized dots at the top corners, with yellow dots added on top straight away. Add three more dots along the bottom of each wing. Add pairs of very large dots on the top and bottom wings. While the dots are still wet, add pink dots on top of the wet aqua dots, so these large spots dry flat.

- Use yellow line icing to add two pairs of medium-sized dots, alongside the body at the top and above the bottom pair of large aqua dots.

- With pink line icing, add three very small dots between the aqua dots along the bottom of the wings, and a curve of three or four dots on the top wing.

- Lastly, use purple line icing to add a row of four purple dots along the top of the wings.

Yellow and purple butterfly

- Outline the butterfly with yellow line icing, flood with the matching icing, then leave to dry completely.

- For the wing pattern, use purple line icing to ice a curvy pattern in the top and bottom segment of each wing. Start and finish each curve with a dot and add pastel lilac glitter straight away, if using.

- With blue line icing, add tiny dots tucked in next to the purple dots at the end of the curves. Also add three dots down the middle of the butterfly, and fill in the triangle sections at the top and bottom, shaping with a

cocktail stick if needed.

- At the very top corners of the wing tips, add a blue dot, with a small pink dot added straight away on top. Add the same dots to the very bottom of the wing tips.

- Add matching sets of three pink dots around the curve edge of the bottom wing sections and at the bottom of the wing tips. With blue, add more sets of dots at the outer edges of the tops of the wings.

Crazy daisies

- I decorated lots of these, using pink, purple, blue, aqua and yellow for various parts of the design. The steps are the same for each.

- Start by outlining and flooding the biscuit, and leaving to dry completely.

- With a second colour, add an outline to the outside and a large dot to the centre. Add glitter straight away, if using.

- When dry, use your third colour to add six lines extending out from the centre. Finish each line with a medium-sized dot. Try to space the lines evenly and have the dots placed in the centre of each petal, so the flower looks symmetrical.

- Between each pair of lines, add two smaller lines with your fourth colour, each with dots at the ends. You will end up with twelve of these smaller lines.

- Finish the daisy by adding four or five small dots in a curve around the edge of each petal, using your fifth colour line icing.

Dragonfly

- The same colours for the butterflies and daisies can be used, in various combinations, for dragonflies. Here is one example.

- With purple line icing, outline the dragonfly's body first. Add an oval-shaped section in the middle and a small round oval at the top, for a head. For the segments, add the second and fourth spots first and then, when dry, add the first and third spots. Spread the dots a little with a cocktail stick so they dry flat. Fill in the head and body with the same line icing, shaking to smooth over.

- Outline the wings with pink line icing. When dry, add the wing detail. Starting at the centre edge, ice four loops, extending each to reach the edge of the wing outline, with aqua line icing. Add jewel ocean spray glitter, if using, while the icing is still wet.

- Finish by giving the dragonfly a pink smile and two eyes: a dot of black on white.

Caterpillar

- Outline the head and body with green line icing. Outline the head section first, extending around the feelers, and then ice each segment one at a time. Add each loop, in turn, to join onto the one in front. With the same icing, fill in the two feeler sections. Leave to dry.

- With purple line icing, fill in each segment. Shake the biscuit when all segments are filled, and add lilac glitter, if using, straight away.

- Finish the caterpillar by adding a line of green for a smile, a dot of black on white for an eye and, with pink line icing, a round spot for a rosy cheek.

Snail

- Outline the snail's head and body with green line icing.

- When dry, add the swirl pattern for the shell, using aqua line icing. Start up near the snail's head, then move into the middle, finishing with a dot. Going round with the bag about three times is about right. Add jewel ocean spray glitter straight away, if using.

- When dry, use purple line icing to add a second swirl, in between the aqua swirl. Finish with a second dot tucked in alongside the aqua dot.

- Add a line of yellow line icing along the bottom of the snail's body. Finish by giving him a pink smile and two eyes: dots of black on white.

Ladybird

- Outline the two wing sections of the ladybird, with black line icing. Add a curve around the top, for the head, and fill in the small tail section at the bottom.

- When dry, flood with red and leave to dry completely.

- Flood the head section with black, and also leave to dry.

- With black flood icing, add dots to the ladybird's wings. Simply squeeze more icing out for bigger dots, and simply touch the nozzle onto the biscuit, for small dots. Circle through the wet spots with a cocktail stick, to spread and flatten them a little.

- With black line icing, add curved feelers, extending out from the head section.

- Finish by adding a small, red mouth and two dots of black on white, for eyes.

BAKING TIP: **BAKING BISCUITS ON STICKS**

Here, I baked some of the butterflies and daisies on sticks, simply because I thought it would be fun to photograph them this way.

This is easy to do, and doesn't need to be limited to this collection. A round circle biscuit baked on a stick can be easily decorated to look like a lollipop, for example.

You can buy special sticks from cake decorating shops, but I prefer simple wooden skewers. They are long and have good pointy ends. If they are too long, cut them to size before using.

When rolling out your biscuit dough, make it about one-centimetre thick. The biscuit needs to be thicker than the thickness of the skewer.

Roll and cut out the biscuits, then push a skewer into them, one by one, after placing on the baking tray. Go slowly when pushing the skewer in. Aim to push in about half the diameter of the biscuit, no less.

Bake the biscuits in a slower oven, 170° Celsius (325° Fahrenheit/gas mark 3). They will need to be in the oven for longer. I start checking at 15 minutes, though they generally take longer. Check every couple of minutes until they are done.

Be prepared for the baking and decorating to take longer. You can't fit as many on a baking tray, so will probably need to bake more batches. When decorating, you need to keep rotating the biscuit, so the stick is not getting in the way of your hand.

THE BUTTERFLY HOUSE

Some butterflies are bright and glittery. These are more restrained and elegant. The matt colours are Wedgwood inspired and the chocolate base certainly makes the finished biscuits look like ceramic tiles. These are the butterflies that appear as gifts for grown-ups or as wedding favours.

The cutters
Butterflies

I have used two different butterfly shapes for this collection, but the simple design is adaptable to any shape.

The biscuits
Chocolate

Icing – line
Pale pink
Cornflower blue
Pale purple
Moss green
Ivory

Icing – flood
Pale pink
Cornflower blue
Pale purple
Moss green

Large butterfly
- Outline the biscuit in your chosen colour of line icing, flood with the same colour and leave to dry.
- When completely dry, add line detail with ivory line icing. Start at the centre of the bottom wing section. Start with a dot, then ice a continuous line to curve around the bottom of the wing, up alongside the centre of the body and then around the top of the wing, finishing with another dot.
- Turn the biscuit upside down and ice the same curved line on the other half, starting and finishing with dots. Add two small line details extending out each way from the centre of the body, finishing each with a small dot.
- For the body segments, fill in the sections at the top and bottom, then add four dots, evenly spaced, down the middle.

Small butterfly
- Outline and flood as for the large butterfly.
- When completely dry, ice two continuous curved lines to add the wing detail, with ivory line icing. Then add dots down the centre, for body segments. Leave to dry.

DESIGN TIP: CHOOSING COMPLEMENTARY COLOURS

These butterflies show how a carefully selected colour palette creates a collection that looks beautiful because, even though the butterfly colours vary, they complement each other, as the tones are evenly matched.

This collection also makes use of another colour secret: ivory. I always have white line icing on the go as it is so useful, but sometimes ivory is a better choice. Whereas white can be bright and stark, ivory is softer and warmer. It is the perfect shade here, but is also a good choice if you are

ever creating wedding biscuits, and know that the bride has opted for ivory over white.

Another useful colour trick is to use slightly contrasting shades of the same colour. Have a look at the purple butterfly in this picture. The icing used to outline and add patterning to the biscuit is a slightly pinker purple than the flood icing. Again, you create a finished biscuit that is effective because the colours complement each other so well.

HIBISCUITS

Sometimes I get ideas for biscuits from completely unlikely sources. I have a skirt that I have worn for years. It is covered with bright hibiscus flowers (it looks prettier than it sounds, honestly). And so, from the skirt, came the hibiscuits. All I had to do was adapt the colours and the designs to make them biscuit-friendly. If you ever wanted to make biscuits for a summer party and you don't have many more cutters other than a set of circle shapes, then these are perfect.

The cutter
Circle shape
(you decide the size)

The biscuits
Vanilla with wholemeal, or chocolate

Icing – line
White

Icing – flood
Pink
Pale blue
Orange
Lime green
If you don't have a colour that is a close match, add a tiny drop of yellow to a leaf green colour.

The hibiscuits

- All the hibiscuits are either chocolate or vanilla. Each is decorated with a combination of either pink-blue, green-blue, pink-orange, orange-blue, green-orange and green-pink colours. Here are the steps to decorate one example.

Pink and orange hibiscuit

- With white line icing, ice the four petals for the hibiscus, making them roughly even in size. Do this by icing the four petals individually, joining up the ends where the petals meet toward the centre. When dry, flood with pink and leave to dry completely.

- Over the top, use white line icing to ice a second lot of smaller petal shapes. Have the petal tips meet nearer the middle. When dry, flood with orange and leave to dry completely.

- From the centre, ice two lines outward per petal, with white line icing. At the tip of each line, create a blob. After icing all eight lines, ice a big blob in the middle of the flower to cover the ends of the lines.

- With lime green line icing, ice tiny dots onto the line ends.

DESIGN TIP: USING ROUND BISCUIT CUTTERS

There is a lot that can be done with a set of round cutters, other than make batches of scones. They offer lots of decorating possibilities. Santa faces and Christmas baubles are two examples (see the It's beginning to look a lot like Christmas collection, on page 161).

When making the hibiscuits, I had plenty of flower cutters

to choose from, but none was the right shape. So I opted for a plain round cutter. All I needed to do was, with a food colour pen, make marks on the biscuit to indicate where to place the four petals. I then iced the four white petals individually, aiming

to make each roughly the same shape and joining the ends where I had made marks on the biscuit. I only needed a couple of practice biscuits to get it right. Once the first petals were outlined and flooded, I had done enough to be able to finish the rest of the flowers.

What made this collection easy was that I had my skirt pattern as my basic design template. If you are developing a design for a round biscuit from scratch, I recommend sketching the design onto paper first, and then marking up your first few biscuits with a food colour pen.

DAD'S TOOLKIT

My father has always maintained that, once married, a man needs a shed, so that hobbies and interests can be protected. A place of refuge against the onslaught that is young children. So, for Father's Day, a collection of biscuit tools is a loving nod to the sanctuary of the shed and all its bits and pieces. Even if Dad's real tools haven't seen to all the DIY tasks over the years, he will enjoy them in biscuit form nevertheless.

The cutters
Screwdriver
Spanner
Hammer
Pliers
Saw

The biscuits
Chocolate

Icing – line
Dark grey
Black
Light brown
Red
Yellow
Dark green

Icing – flood
Light grey
Red
Black

Screwdriver
- Outline the handle section with red line icing, flood with red and leave to dry.
- Use dark green line icing to fill in the top section of the handle and leave to dry.
- Outline the top section with dark grey line icing and, when dry, flood with light grey flood icing. When dry, outline again with dark grey line icing, and add a second line parallel to the outline, to emphasise the shape. Make the line across the very top quite thick, to show the chiselled edge.
- Finish by adding four or five straight lines down the handle, using yellow line icing.

Spanner
- Outline the biscuit with dark grey line icing, flood with light grey and leave to dry.
- Outline the biscuit again with dark grey line icing, to give the spanner definition and to show the various sections.

Hammer
- With dark grey line icing, outline the top section of the hammer, and flood with light grey icing. Leave to dry.
- Outline the handle section with black line icing, flood and leave to dry. When dry, outline and add diagonal grip markings, using dark green line icing.
- Around the head of the hammer, add line detail with dark grey line icing.

Pliers
- Outline the handles with red line icing, then flood with red. When dry, outline and add diagonal grip markings, using yellow line icing.

- When dry, outline the top sections with dark grey line icing, leaving a section for the teeth. Flood with light grey and leave to dry.
- Add detail with dark grey line icing. For the teeth, add evenly spaced small dots along each edge of the plier jaws, then tease each dot to a point with a cocktail stick. Fill in the two small curved cutting sections near where the jaws join together. Add a circle of grey to represent a screw head, and then outline the outside of the two sections.

Saw

- Outline the blade section with dark grey line icing, flood with light grey and leave to dry.
- For the handle, outline with light brown and, when dry, fill with the same icing. Shake to smooth the surface. Leave to dry.
- Add a yellow dot for a brass screw head. Add lines of dark grey on every second tooth, to emphasise the serrated saw edge.

HOME IS WHERE THE HEART IS

A housewarming present with a difference. And while, when moving house, most people aren't moving into a country cottage, I think decorating biscuits in this style is entirely appropriate. It suggests cosiness and comfort. Home rather than house. This collection also demonstrates the versatility of biscuits as gifts. These particular ones were not made as a housewarming gift at all, but for a 90th birthday, for a man who had a long career as a painter and decorator.

The cutters
House
Numbers

The biscuits
Gingerbread

Icing – line
Yellow
Blue
Brick
Made by adding a drop of brown to burgundy.
Brown
Skintone or very light brown
Red
Green
Sand
Made by mixing brown into yellow.
Black
White

Icing – flood
Yellow
Blue
Brick
Sand
White
Red

Blue cottage
- Outline the main front part of the house with blue line icing. Be careful to make sure the lines for the roof are even and meet in the centre. Mark your biscuit with a food colour pen if you need to. Flood with blue and leave to dry completely.
- Outline the section at the top of the house for the roof, using brick line icing. Outline the chimney when the roof outline is dry, leaving a section clear at the top. Flood both sections with brick icing.
- For the door, outline with yellow line icing, then flood. When dry, ice three yellow lines, to indicate wood panels.
- Ice three squares for windows, using black line icing, and fill with the same icing. When completely dry, ice window shutters using yellow line icing. Make the outline first, then fill with the same icing.

When dry, use white line icing to ice straight lines over the window, to make the panes.
- For the bricked chimney, outline and fill a section at the top with skintone icing (which happens to be a good colour for mortar), or light brown. Then ice three horizontal lines evenly across the chimney, then a series of vertical lines between them to mark the bricks.
- Finish the house by adding a black dot, for a doorknob.

Thatched cottage
- Outline the house front with white line icing before flooding with white. As for the blue cottage, mark the point where the lines meet in the centre, if you are not confident doing this by eye.
- Outline the roof section with sand line icing, then flood. Using the sand line icing, add some thatch. Leave each set of lines that you ice to dry

before adding more, so they stay distinct and don't run together.

- Outline the chimney in brick line icing, leaving a section at the top. Flood with brick.

- Outline a square door with red line icing, before flooding red. Ice two squares for windows, using black line icing, and fill with the same icing. When completely dry, ice green window boxes underneath, using green line icing. Outline the box shape first, then fill with the same icing. When dry, use white line icing to ice straight lines over the window, to make the panes.

- Add an eave over the door in green line icing, in the same way as for the window boxes.

- For the gables, use brown line icing and add the straight lines first. Make tiny scratch marks in the white icing with a pin or cocktail stick to mark out the line ends first, if you are not confident doing the lines by eye. Fill with the same icing, giving the biscuit a shake to smooth over.

- For the brickwork on the chimney, outline and fill a section at the top with skintone or light brown icing. Then ice two or three horizontal lines evenly across

the chimney, then a series of vertical lines between them to mark the bricks.

- Finish the house by adding a black dot, for a doorknob.

Numbers

- Outline your chosen number, or numbers, with brick line icing, then fill with brick flood icing. Leave to dry completely.

- Add the lines for the mortar markings in the same way as on the chimneys. Ice a series of evenly spaced horizontal lines first, using skintone or light brown line icing. Then add vertical lines between the horizontal lines. Space them evenly.

COMMOTION IN THE OCEAN

A wonderful collection in that you can make it as bright, colourful and sparkly as you like. You can decorate some realistically – as much as a biscuit allows – such as the dolphin, but, for me, the urge to go Technicolor and to create a cast of characters that might turn up in an animated movie was overwhelming. The starfish are some of my favourite biscuits in the book, which is all down to their crazy colours. I also have a soft spot for the sparkly pink seahorse, as I made these for my daughter's 'commotion in the ocean'-themed second birthday party. And if you are looking for a party theme for a young child, it is okay to base your choice on what biscuits you want to make. Works for me.

The cutters
Dolphin
Starfish
Tropical fish
Scallop shell
Angel fish
Blue whale
Seahorse
Shark
Clownfish
You may have shapes that differ slightly from mine. Just adapt the colours and the designs to suit.

The biscuits
Vanilla with wholemeal, or chocolate

Icing – line
Dolphin blue
Made by mixing drops of sky blue and cornflower blue.
Aqua
Yellow
Pink
Royal blue
Ivory
White
Fuchsia

Orange
Purple
Turquoise
Black
A selection of bright, fun colours for the scallop shells and starfish

Icing – flood
Dolphin blue
Aqua
Yellow
Pink
Royal blue
Ivory
Orange
Pale turquoise
Made by adding drops of white to turquoise.
Colours to match the line icing for the scallop shells and starfish

Optional glitter
Pastel yellow
Pastel pink
Lavender
Jewel oasis blue

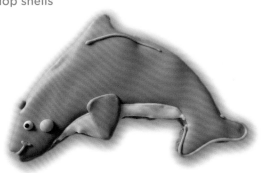

Dolphin

- Outline the main part of the dolphin's body with dolphin blue line icing, then flood. Leave a section at the bottom of the biscuit for a white underbelly.

- When dry, outline the belly with white line icing, then fill with the same icing.

When the biscuit is completely dry, add a flipper. Outline in dolphin blue, then fill with the same icing. Then add dolphin blue line details: an outline on the tail, a line to indicate the curve of the dolphin's back, a dot for a blowhole and a smile.

Finish by adding an eye – a black dot on a white dot – and pink dot for a rosy cheek.

working in. Add a mix of small, medium and large dots. Leave the centre of the biscuit spot-free. Leave to dry.

When dry, add the starfish's face. Add dots of black on dots of white for eyes, a small curve of ivory line icing for a mouth, and two dots of pink for rosy cheeks.

orange lines. Feather the lines with a cocktail stick, dragging lightly toward the tail end. Be sure to feather along the ends of the lines, to create an even edge. Leave to dry.

Outline the fins and tail with aqua line icing before flooding. When dry, add line details. A line along the edge of each fin, and four or five lines along the tail.

Finish the fish by adding an eye – black dot on white – a pink dot for a rosy cheek and a tiny pink dot for a mouth.

Starfish

Here are the steps to decorate a purple starfish with ivory spots, but the process is the same, whatever colours you choose.

Outline the whole starfish with purple line icing, then flood. While the icing is still wet, add dots of ivory line icing. Do one arm at a time, starting at the tip and

Tropical fish

Outline an oval shape in the middle of the biscuit for the body, using yellow line icing.

Flood the body with yellow. While the icing is still wet, add straight lines down the body in some bright colours. I used alternate aqua and

Scallop shell

Here are the steps to decorate a purple scallop shell. The steps are the same for any chosen colour.

Outline the biscuit with purple line icing, then flood.

Along the bottom of the shell, outline the rectangular edge, and add a curved line, using ivory line icing. Add pastel yellow glitter, if using. Brush off the excess when dry.

For the dots, ice small dots, using ivory line icing, in two stages. First, ice every second dot, around the edge and in five lines down the shell. Work reasonably quickly if you want a glittery shell as small dots can dry quickly. Add glitter if using, leave to dry, then brush off the excess.

- Then add the second lot of dots, in between the first, and add another lot of glitter, if using. Brush off the excess when dry.

Angel fish

- Outline the whole biscuit with ivory line icing.

- When dry, flood with ivory. While the icing is still wet, add three thick lines of aqua flood icing down the fish's body. For this I switched my usual number 4 nozzle for a bigger number 6, to get the line thickness. Another way to do it is to snip across the hole in your aqua line icing bag, to make a bigger hole, remembering that after you have added the thick lines you will need to transfer your remaining icing into a new

bag. Use a cocktail stick to neaten edges of the lines, if needed. Leave to dry.

- Add aqua line details. On the tail, add four or five lines. Ice a shape for a fin in the middle of the fish and add four or five lines within the shape. Add a small fin shape at the bottom of the fish and a small line at the top of the first thick line of aqua, to create a tapered effect.

- Finish by adding a dot of black on a dot of white for an eye, a dot of ivory line icing for a mouth and a dot of pink for a rosy cheek.

Blue whale

- With royal blue line icing, outline the whale's body, leaving a section at the bottom for an underbelly. Flood with royal blue. If you want a glittery whale, add a generous amount of Jewel oasis blue glitter and leave to dry, before brushing off the excess.

- Use white line icing to fill in the small section at the bottom of the whale.

- When dry, use royal blue line icing to add a flipper. Outline the shape, then fill in straight away. Use the same icing to add a smile, and a dot for a blowhole. Ice a line along the bottom of the whale, where the blue meets the white.

- Finish with a dot of black on white, for an eye, and a pink dot for a rosy cheek, if you like.

Turquoise seahorse

- With turquoise line icing, outline the main body of the seahorse, leaving sections for the fins and belly. The tricky part here is doing the curly tail in one line. Practise on your worktop, or draw a faint line on the biscuit with a food colour pen. Flood with pale turquoise.

- With yellow, outline the belly, then flood. With line icing, add a series of dots down the back of the seahorse, making the dots at the end smaller. If you want to use glitter, add it now and leave to dry, before brushing off.

- Outline the two fins with purple, then fill with the same icing. If you want to use glitter, sprinkle it on when the icing is wet and brush off the excess when dry.

- Use purple line icing to add line detail to the fins. Outline the belly section again with yellow line icing and add four or five curved horizontal lines across the belly.

- With turquoise line icing, ice along the jawline, making the line thicker at the tip for a nose.

- Add a black dot on white for an eye, and a pink dot for a rosy cheek. Seahorses are shy creatures, so I think they need to be blushing.

Pink seahorse

- With pink line icing, outline the main body of the seahorse, leaving sections for the fins and belly. Flood with pink. If you want a sparkly seahorse, pile on the pastel pink glitter, leave to dry and then brush off the excess.

- With yellow line icing, outline the belly section and flood. Using the same yellow line icing, outline and then fill a small triangular fin on the head. When the belly is dry, outline again and add three or four curved horizontal lines across the belly.

- Outline the main fin around the head with purple, then fill with the same icing. Add a second small purple fin in the middle of the body, in the same way. With fuchsia line icing, outline the fin at the back and fill straight away. When all the fins have dried, add line detail. For this seahorse, I have added very light, feathery lines in alternate directions. If needed, the ends of the lines can be tapered with a cocktail stick.

- Finish the seahorse by adding a black dot on white for an eye and a line of pink line icing along the jawline.

Whale shark

- With dolphin blue line icing, outline the shark's body, including the fin at the bottom. Leave small sections either side of this fin, for the white underbelly.

- Flood with dolphin blue and, while wet, ice on a random pattern of very small white dots, with white line icing. While wet, drag a cocktail stick through some of the dots around the middle of the shark, toward the tail, to create a streamlined effect. Leave to dry.

- With white line icing, fill in the belly section at the bottom of the shark.

- When dry, add line details. Three vertical lines on the shark's cheek for gills and three lines along the shark's body, meeting at a point near the tail.

- Finish with a dot of black on a dot of white, for the shark's eye. He doesn't need teeth – whale sharks don't have any.

Clownfish

- Outline the whole biscuit with orange line icing, flood with orange, then leave to dry.

- Add thick white lines. I did this by icing outlines first with white line icing, filling straight away with the same icing, and then shaking the biscuit to smooth over.

- Next add line detail with orange line icing. Slanted lines for the fins at the top and bottom, seven or eight horizontal lines on the tailfin and two oval-ish blobs for a fleshy, fishy mouth. Outline a small fin shape in the middle of the fish and add two or three lines within the shape.

- With black line icing, outline the edge of the white stripes, and add lines along the edges of all the fins.

- Finish by adding a dot of black on white, for an eye.

DECORATING TIP: **FLAT DOTS AND RAISED DOTS**

In this collection, I have used two dot techniques. On the starfish, I added the spots of icing while the base flood colour was still wet. This means that, when the icing dries, you get a flat finish.

On the scallop shells, I took a different approach. I waited until the base flood icing was completely dry, then added lots of small tiny dots. I had to do this in two lots, to avoid the dots running together while the icing was wet. So, I added every second dot first, leaving a small gap in between each one. I then added pastel yellow glitter while the icing was still wet. After the dots were dry and I had brushed off the excess glitter, I repeated the process, adding the second lot of dots between the first lot of dry, glittery dots.

With the starfish, I chose the flat dot technique as I wanted to evoke the bubbles washing around the starfish as the seawater runs over the sand. With the scallop, I went for raised dots so they could stand proud of the flat shell, and become the main decorative feature. If dots of icing are added to a dried flood base, then you also have the glitter option, which you can't do with the flat dots technique. I like to think this is the sort of glittery scallop you might find in a mermaid's hair.

While being able to use glitter is a big plus to the raised dot technique, the big advantage when opting for flat dots is the time saved. As you are adding the dots when the flood icing is still wet, this is obviously much quicker than if you were waiting for it to dry. The bulk of the decorating for each starfish is done in one phase. With the scallop shells, I have to be honest, adding all those tiny dots in two stages did take a long time. But then, I love the finish.

Whichever dot method you choose is up to you. Experiment. Creating different effects using simple techniques is a big part of the fun of biscuit decorating.

TIME FOR TREATS

Summers in the UK have a habit of being a bit of a washout. While we all wish desperately for glorious sunshine, we still pack umbrellas for our August beach holidays. Just in case. It was during one of these below-average summers, weather-wise, that I made a huge collection of ice cream biscuits – to provide the taste and colours of summer, in the absence of sunshine. If you ever wish to make biscuits for a child with a summer birthday, can I suggest these?

The cutters
Ice cream

The biscuits
Vanilla with wholemeal

Icing – line
Light beige
Made by adding drops of yellow, orange and brown, then lightening with white.
Creamy vanilla
Made by adding the tiniest drop of yellow to ivory icing.
Brown
White
A selection of bright, cheerful colours of your choice
I have used pink, purple, aqua and red.

Icing – flood
Flood icing to match your chosen line icing
Here, I used creamy vanilla, brown, pink, purple, aqua and red.

Optional glitter and decorations
Glitter colours of your choice
I used blue, pink and purple pastel.
A range of sprinkles and decorations
Coloured dragees, chocolate strands, white chocolate stars. Whatever catches your eye in the cake decorating section of your supermarket.

Ice creams
- All the ice creams are decorated in the same way. The cones are identical and each has a chocolate or vanilla bottom scoop of ice cream, followed by a contrasting colour for the top scoop, with some form of sprinkles or glitter added to the top colour.

- Here I describe how I decorated two ice creams. The final choice of colours and sprinkles is up to you. As you can see from the main photograph, there are endless variations on this theme. If it helps, line up all your icing colours and your pots of glitter and sprinkles on your workbench before you start decorating, and write down what you think are good matches.

Cherry chocolate ice cream

- Outline the cone in light beige. First, ice a horizontal, narrow oval shape, for the top of the cone. Next, add lines diagonally across the cone, taking care to space them evenly. Leave the biscuit to dry for a few minutes, then turn the biscuit around and add another set of diagonal lines, to create a diamond pattern. Fill in the bottom section of the cone to create a small, solid triangle.

- Outline the bottom scoop of ice cream in brown. You don't need to follow a specific pattern for each ice cream, just make sure you ice lots of curves and drips, so the ice cream is looking like it is just starting to melt. Ice a drip or two down the cone. When dry, flood with brown and leave to dry.

- For the top scoop, outline in red, again curving the icing line to give a just-melting effect. When dry, flood with red. While the icing is still wet, add glitter or sprinkles that complement the icing. I have used pink and white dragees here.

Grape vanilla ice cream

- Decorate the cone section in the same way as for the cherry chocolate ice cream.

- Outline the bottom scoop of ice cream in vanilla colour icing, again adding curves and drips, including one or two down the cone. When dry, flood with the same vanilla colour.

- Add a drippy, curvy outline for the top scoop in purple, and flood with the same colour. I then gently pushed some white chocolate stars into the still-wet purple icing, before leaving to dry.

DECORATING TIP: STOCKING UP ON SPRINKLES

Don't think that the little containers of sprinkles that can be bought at the supermarket aren't fancy or specialist enough for your biscuits, they can be very versatile.

Just don't go overboard and buy everything, thinking you will end up using it. I have a little pot of elephant-shaped sprinkles that really needs to have its use-by date checked. I just simply haven't had a call for them.

Instead, buy simple sprinkles that can be used in many ways. My most oft-used sprinkles are easily dragees. The silver balls, particularly. They can become decorations on Christmas trees, gems on crowns, bells on collars, all sorts of things. Chocolate strands are also useful – for sprinkling on tree trunks and for animal fur. I am also a big fan of the white chocolate stars used in this collection. And the pots of tiny, tiny multi-coloured balls, what we as children called 'hundreds and thousands' are perfect for the ice creams here and for sprinkling on cupcake toppings (see Vintage tea party, page 55).

And needless to say, if you are decorating with children, the type and colour of the sprinkles don't matter. They will all be used equally and applied abundantly.

WE'RE GOING TO THE CHAPEL

While decorated biscuits of any kind are wonderful, wedding biscuits can be really special. Pure white always looks classic and the symbols of marriage are easily found in biscuit cutter form. Your decorated wedding biscuits could be favours for guests, place settings or, as in this case, a gift for a newly married couple. Here comes the bride...

The cutters

Bride and groom
Heart
Ring
Church
Wedding cake
Wedding dress

You can buy specific bride and groom cutters. I don't really like them. For me, the gingerbread man and woman fit the bill perfectly for this collection. They make a fun bride and groom, and using these shapes gets you out of having to try to ice lifelike faces on each.

The biscuits

Vanilla with wholemeal, or chocolate

Icing – line

White
Yellow
Dark, forest green
Red
Grey
Pale blue
Pale pink
Black
Brown

Icing – flood

White
Black

Icing – rosettes

Red
Avocado green

Optional glitter

White
Gold

Bride

- Outline the basic shape for the bride's dress with white line icing and, when dry, flood with white.

- If you want to add white glitter to your bride, you need to do this in stages. This will allow the icing to dry and the dots and other details to keep their shape, without the risk of them running into any other wet icing.

- For the first stage, use white line icing to add two white dots to either side of the bride's head, a line across her bust, a curved line along the bottom of her dress and two dots, evenly spaced, on the edge of each of her sleeves. Also add half the dots along the neckline of her dress, leaving sufficient space between each one for the second batch of dots. While this icing is still wet, shake a load of white glitter over it all, wait until completely dry and then brush off the excess.

- For the second lot of white detail, again using the same line icing, add two smaller dots underneath the two dots on her head, to make earrings, two more dots in between the existing dots on her sleeves, bows to the bottom of her dress, the second lot of dots around her neckline and half the dots underneath the bodice seam, with space in between each for the second half of the dots. Pile on the white glitter again and then brush off when dry.

- To finish the detail on her dress, add the last lot of dots to the line under the bodice seam, add white glitter, and brush off when dry.

- For the bride's hair ice a curve along the top of her head and then two curves along her forehead to meet in the middle, using brown line icing. (Brown was used as this is the hair colour of the bride, Claire.) Leave to dry before adding a couple more brown lines. Leave to dry again before finishing with a couple more lines. Leaving the icing to dry this way will leave you with distinct hair-like icing, rather than having all the icing run together and smooth over.

- Lastly, give her a happy face. Use pink line icing to give her rosy cheeks and a smile. Ice a dot of black on top of a dot of white for her eyes.

Groom
- Outline the basic shape for the groom's suit with black, leaving a section for his shirt and waistcoat, and keeping his hands uniced. Flood with black and leave to dry.

- Fill in the section between his suit front with grey line icing, giving the biscuit a shake to smooth over.

- When dry, fill in the section above his waistcoat with white, for his shirt, and leave to dry again.

- Ice the groom's hair in the same way as the bride's. Outline the hair shape and then add lines of brown, leaving the lines to dry before adding more.

- Using pale blue line icing, ice a shape for a tie and add a blue line at the bottom of his waistcoat for a cummerbund. Add lines of white across his feet and at the end of his suit sleeves, for socks and shirt cuffs.

- Create a small rosette on his suit using red rosette icing (see Decorating tip: Romantic rosettes, on page 55). When the red rosette is dry, add two small green leaves on either side.

- Give him his smile and rosy cheeks in the same way as the bride's, using pink line icing. Then ice two dots of white followed by two dots of black, for eyes.

Church

- Outline the whole of the church shape with white line icing, flood with white and leave to dry.

- Add details with forest green line icing. Outline the door and eaves and fill straight away, and ice a line for the window sill. Shake the biscuit to smooth over.

- When dry, add red details. Fill in the steeple, and outline and fill the roof with the same red. Give the biscuit a quick shake to smooth over. Add lines over the door with brown line icing, adding two brown dots for door handles.

- Lastly, use white line icing to ice a shape for a window on the side of the church, and a window above the door. If you like, add white glitter, shaking off the excess when dry.

Wedding ring

- Using yellow line icing, outline the main, circular outside of the ring. Ice a smaller circle inside this, to create an outline for a band. Then ice an outline for a claw at the top, and fill in all these parts with the same line icing. A quick shake will smooth over the surface.

- While the yellow icing is still wet, add a lot of gold glitter to cover the icing. Leave to dry, then shake off the excess.

- Lastly, fill in the section at the top with white line icing to create a diamond, and add white glitter. Leave to dry before shaking off the excess.

Wedding dress

- Outline the whole biscuit with white line icing and flood with white. Leave to dry.

- Using white line icing, ice three of the six dots underneath the bust, leaving space between each one. In the same way, ice half the dots along the top bustline, leaving a space between each one. Ice two lines along the bottom of the dress, following the curves at the bottom of the biscuit. For the dot pattern on the skirt, ice the dots evenly in a diamond arrangement. I started with three dots under the bust, then spaced the rest from there. If you are using white glitter, shake it all over the dress, leave to dry and then brush off the excess.

- Add the second lot of dots in between the existing dots along the top of the bustline and underneath the bust, add glitter if using, and shake off when dry.

Wedding cake

- Outline the whole biscuit with white line icing and flood with white. Leave to dry.

- Using white line icing, ice seven lines across the sections of the cake, to distinguish the tiers. Then ice a scallop pattern underneath four of the lines, adding extra

scallop sections for each tier. I have iced a 2-5-6-7 pattern. Ice six dots along the bottom of the cake. Add white glitter while wet, leave to dry, then brush off.

- Ice a heart shape with white line icing at the top, flood and then cover with white glitter. I then iced small white dots around the outside of the heart. If you like, you now have room to add the initials of the bride and groom.

- Add small rosettes along each row of scallop section. I have iced a 1-4-5-6 arrangement. Leave the rosettes to dry before adding two green lines to each one, for leaves.

His 'n' her hearts

- For this collection, I made a heart each for Rich and Claire, the newlyweds. No apologies for sticking with pink for hers and blue for his. These are the steps to decorate Rich's heart, but the process is the same for both. Note that I used chocolate biscuits here, as I don't think you get the right colour contrast between biscuit and icing if you use vanilla.

- Write the name first, using pale blue line icing, spacing

it evenly across the widest part of the heart.

- Add the rosettes. Space the rosettes evenly. I put one on either side of the groom's name, one in the middle under his name, and then spaced the others from there. When the rosettes are dry, add green leaves, two to each rosette. Partially

rotating the biscuit here and there as you add the leaves will create a random effect.

- Add small dots in pale blue line icing between each rosette, then outline the whole heart in the same pale blue.

DECORATING TIP: **LETTERING MADE EASY**

I must confess that, when I started out decorating biscuits, I put off trying writing for a long time. It really looked like a super-advanced skill. Part of me still thinks it is, because I have never been very good at doing fancy, calligraphic writing using royal icing.

I got over my fears by coming up with a simple lettering technique instead, that anyone can do.

The secret is the big dots at the start and end of each letter. When you start your first letter, let's say 'C', start by squeezing out a dot. Without stopping, then move the icing bag around and create the semi-circle for the 'C'. At the spot where you want to finish, stop moving and squeeze another dot at the end of the letter.

Starting and ending this way gives you more control. You get to start and finish your letter slowly and deliberately, giving you time to focus, and the dots make sure each letter has a neat finish. No scraggly ends or trailing bits of icing. Genius.

WHAT'S NEW PUSSYCAT?

A cat-shaped cutter is very versatile. I have three, but even one shape iced with different colours and patterns will create a varied collection of colourful kitties. The temptation, of course, is to let your designs be influenced by cats of past, as I was. And so we have my Grandmother's Siamese, Chota, Eric my black and white moggy, Pumpkin the very friendly calico and lastly a marmalade tabby, which demanded inclusion as mother's family always seem to acquire them, and they all somehow end up being called Charlie.

The cutters
A selection of cats

The biscuits
Chocolate and vanilla with wholemeal

Icing – line
Black
Ivory
White
Delphinium blue
Yellow-orange
Made by adding drops of yellow and brown to orange, then lightening with white.
Orange
Pink
Green

Icing – flood
Black
White
Ivory
Delphinium blue
Yellow-orange
Orange

Notes on colours
I have used a particular colour for the Siamese cat's points – delphinium blue – yet these cats come in many shades. Lilac, grey and chocolate colours will all work for the cat's points.
The orange colour has a small amount of copper, to make it look a bit more brownish and natural. Straight orange is too bright.

Black and white
- Outline the whole body of the cat in black line icing. When dry, flood with black.
- Straight away, put a good dollop of white flood onto the wet black at the points of the cat – feet, tail, face. With a cocktail stick, drag through each blob of white three or four times to turn the white blobs into fur.

Wipe your cocktail stick on a clean piece of kitchen towel after each drag through the icing, so that you don't get spots of black in the white.
- Allow to dry before adding eyes, a nose and ear detail.

Siamese
- Outline the cat's body with ivory line icing, leaving the points. When the ivory has dried, outline the points with delphinium blue, or your chosen colour.

- When dry, flood with ivory and, at the same time, flood the point areas with delphinium blue. Use a cocktail stick to bring the two colours to meet.

- Allow to dry before adding eyes, a nose and ear detail.

Calico

- Use your three line colours – orange, black and white - to outline the biscuits. There aren't any rules as to where to put the colours, simply put some of each around the edge of the biscuit. Just let the icing dry between applying each colour.

- When dry, flood one biscuit at a time. Flood with each colour in turn, alongside the same colour outline, to create sections of colour on the cat. Use a cocktail stick to draw the icing colours together and close any gaps.

- Allow to dry before adding eyes, a nose and ear detail.

Marmalade tabby

- Outline with yellow-orange line icing, leaving gaps for the cat's chin, feet, stomach and tail. When dry, outline these areas with white line icing.

- Flood with yellow-orange for the main part of the cat, and with white for the cat's white sections. Use a cocktail stick to bring the two colours together.

- Straight away, use orange flood icing to add stripes along the cat's body. Make sure your icing tip is wide enough to create quite thick stripes. I use a no. 4 tip. While the icing is still wet, drag the ends with a cocktail stick to create tapered stripes.

- When dry, add eyes, a nose and ear detail.

Eyes, nose and ears

- Regardless of the colours used, the method is the same for all of the cats' eyes. A dot of coloured line icing for the iris followed straight away by a small dot of black line icing. I gave the marmalade and calico cats green eyes, the black and white cat a white eye, and the Siamese the same blue as his points.

- For the nose, apply a dot of your chosen colour, then tease the ends with a cocktail stick to spread it a little. This gives the nose definition, rather than leaving it looking like a coloured dot. I gave all my cats little pink noses, except for the Siamese, who has a black nose.

- For ear detail, simply pipe a small amount of line colour around the edges of the ears.

DECORATING TIP: **FLOODING WITH MORE THAN ONE COLOUR**

With these cats, a lot of the pattern effects were created by flooding with different colours at the same time. This is a great decorating technique – you can get the same flat finish as when flooding with one colour, but you don't have to wait for one colour to dry before adding the next.

First, outline your biscuits in your chosen colours. Allow a short time to dry between each colour. Be sure to start and finish your lines of colour in the right spots, such as the start and finish of a cat's tail, for example.

Then flood, one colour at a time. Use a generous amount, but don't worry too much about getting total coverage at this point. Just squeeze the icing colours onto the biscuit in roughly the areas you want them, aiming to get the different colours close together where they are to meet.

When you have added all your colours, reach for your high-tech accessory: the cocktail stick. Gently push and draw the sections of icing together so that the wet edges meet. As soon as the colours touch, you are done.

A gentle shake of the biscuit on the worktop will smooth out any dimples or undulations caused by the cocktail stick. Make sure to wipe the cocktail stick clean of icing after each 'drag', as otherwise you could add dots of one colour into another, messing up your otherwise neat finish.

Leave your biscuit to dry before adding any finishing details.

PEDIGREE POOCHES

If asked whether one is a cat person or a dog person, a definitive answer is required. It is difficult to get away with saying "both". One must pledge an oath of loyalty to the chosen species, akin to the level of devotion offered a football team, and forsake all other animals. I guess the fact that our house has two cats and is dog-free gives away my allegiance but, having made a cats collection, I simply had to make a dog collection. For fairness, and because they are simply adorable. And I don't think my cats will mind if I confess that I had more fun making these than the moggies.

The cutters
Labrador/dalmatian
Schnauzer
Dachshund
Poodle
Scottie

The biscuits
Vanilla with wholemeal

Icing – line
White
Black
Pink
Golden brown
Made by adding a tiny drop of brown to buttercup yellow.
Light brown
Grey
Red
Line icing for the scottie's blanket
Here, I used dark green, navy blue, golden brown and black.

Icing – flood
Black
White
Golden brown
Pink
Grey

Golden labrador

- While a golden labrador is shown here, you can also make brown or black dogs.
- Using golden brown line icing, outline the whole dog, then flood. Leave to dry.
- Outline an ear and fill with the same golden brown line icing. Use a cocktail stick to shape, if needed.
- Add a thickish line of red line icing for a collar. With black line icing, add three black lines on each foot, for claws.

Add a dot of black for a nose, and extend the line to make a wide curved mouth.

- Finish the labrador by adding a black square line section on his collar, to make a buckle, and by adding a dot of black on white, for an eye.

Dalmatian

- Outline with white line icing, then flood. While the icing is still wet, add very small splodges of black, using line icing. Make the splodges random and uneven, but make sure none of them is too big. Try not to add too much black for any one splodge, to minimise colour bleed. Leave to dry.
- With white line icing, add an ear in the same way as for the labrador. Add a few black splodges.

- With red line icing, add a collar. When dry, add a small black line section, for a buckle.
- With black line icing, add three claws on each foot and a nose. Extend the icing from the nose to make a smile.
- Finish the dalmatian with an eye: a dot of black on white.

Schnauzer

- With white line icing outline sections on the outside of the biscuit for feet, muzzle and ears. With grey line icing, outline the rest of the dog's body.
- Fill in the white sections with the same icing and flood the rest of the biscuit with grey. Use a cocktail stick to feather the sections together. Leave to dry.

- Add a thickish line of red, for a collar. When dry, add small black lines to make a buckle and use the same black to add a dot for a nose. Extend a line from the nose upward to make a smile.
- Use white line icing to outline the ear tips and add a dot of black on white, for an eye.

Dachshund

- With light brown line icing, outline sections on the edge of the biscuit for feet and muzzle. Outline the remaining parts of the biscuit with black line icing.

- Fill the light brown sections with the same icing, and flood the main part with black. Flood right up to the edges of the brown so that the two colours are just touching. Leave to dry.

- Outline a long, floppy ear with black line icing, then fill with the same icing and shake to smooth over.

- Add three black lines for claws, on each foot, and a black dot for a nose, extending a line from the nose to make a smile.

- Finish with a dot of black on white, for an eye.

Poodle

- Outline the whole biscuit with pink line icing, then flood with pink and leave to dry.

- For the pompoms, use pink line icing to outline a daisy-ish shape on the tail and feet.

- Outline a similar section on the head, for the fur there. You don't need to be too precise, just make sure you do a scallop edge. Within these outlines, make little swirls with the same pink icing, to represent curly fur. Add just enough to fill in the outline. Don't add too much or the icing will start to run together.

- Add tiny lines of black at the bottom of the feet and a tiny black nose. Add a dot of black on white, for an eye.

- If you would like your poodles to have pearls, add three or four tiny dots in white, along her neck, leaving a small space between each one. Leave them to dry, then add another three or four dots in between the first dots.

Scottie

- Outline the whole biscuit with black line icing, then flood with black and leave to dry.
- Add a thickish line of red, with line icing, for a collar.
- With dark green line icing, ice a square over the dog's back, fill with the same colour, and shake to smooth. Leave to dry. With navy blue line icing, add a series of straight lines over the green. I did two pairs of horizontal rows, and three pairs of vertical rows. Leave to dry. Finish the blanket by adding lines of black: two horizontal lines and three vertical lines.
- Add a dot for a nose, with the line extended to make a curvy mouth. Add black line detail around the ears and on the collar.
- Finish by adding a dot of black on white, for an eye.

DECORATING TIP: **EASY ON THE EYES**

All throughout this book you will see the instruction: "Add a dot of black on white, for an eye." It sounds so simple but, when I first started biscuit decorating, it actually took a bit of experimentation to get animal eyes right.

You see, I was quite paranoid about colour bleed, having run into this problem a few times on my first decorating attempts. And colour

bleed can always be more of a problem when dark icing is next to light, such as black and white. I didn't want all my animals to look like they had cataracts.

So, for a while, I added a white dot and then added a second dot of black only when the first dot was completely dry. But I realised that I had to come up with something else when I delivered a batch of biscuits to a café and found tiny spots of black icing scattered on the base underneath the glass dome that displayed my biscuits: by adding the black dots to dried white dots, I was creating very raised up eyes and the black pupils were getting knocked off.

I then tried a black food colour pen. I let the white dots dry, then drew on a black circle for a pupil. They looked great, but after about a day, the black dots faded to grey. So that wasn't the solution, either.

By this stage, I was beginning to crack the colour bleed problem (see Help! My biscuit has... on page 186) and got enough confidence to add a black dot straight on top of the wet dot of white icing. It worked. Have a look at the close up of this poodle's face: you can see that the dot of black has dried flat on top of the dot of white, with no colour bleed.

The secret, if you can call it that, is in the quality and consistency of the icing. Make sure it is well mixed and the line icing, particularly the black, is not at all runny and that you only add the tiniest dot, so that it doesn't flow into the white or sink down into it, but stays on top.

So, when you see an icing instruction for an eye, you can add a dot of black on top of a dot of white, straight away.

DOWN ON THE FARM

On our family farm in Western Australia, what you get are huge paddocks of golden wheat, dense flocks of merinos, dry dams and feisty sheepdogs. Things are very different on the biscuit farm. This is the farm of children's storybooks, where the fields are small and green and all the animals live happily alongside each other. The rooster crows every morning, lambs frolic, it is eternally spring and the farmer's name is Macdonald.

The cutters
- Sheep
- Cow
- Rooster
- Hen
- Goose
- Pig

The biscuits
- Vanilla with wholemeal

Icing – line
- Light brown
- Pink
- Red
- Dark brown
- Burgundy
- Dark green
- Orange
- Golden brown
  Made by adding a tiny drop of brown to buttercup yellow.
- Orange-brown
  Made by adding a drop of brown to orange.
- Grey
- Black
- White

Icing – flood
- Light brown
- Pink
- Dark brown
- Orange-brown
- Black
- White

Rooster
- With red line icing, outline and fill the comb section first, and leave to dry. With burgundy line icing, add a round section under the comb, where the eye will be added later.

- Outline three sections, using line icing. Outline a light brown head and chest around the outside of the biscuit only, leaving a section for the wattle. Then, outline a dark brown body and finish the outlining with a black tail. Leave a section at the bottom for the feet.

- Flood all three colours in succession, working quickly. Bring the edges of the flood icing together with a cocktail stick. While the icing is wet, add small dots of line icing: grey on the light brown, light brown on the dark brown body and dark green on the tail. With a cocktail stick, drag through the dots to gently marble. Wipe the cocktail stick clean after each drag. Leave to dry.

- With red line icing, fill in one part of the wattle. Add the second part when the first is dry, so the icing keeps its shape. Fill in a beak section with golden brown line icing.

- For the feet, use golden brown line icing to add tiny lines. Allow one foot to dry, before adding the second.

- Finish by adding a dot of black on burgundy, for an eye.

Hen
- Outline the biscuit with white line icing, leaving sections

for the beak and feet. Flood with white and leave to dry.

- Fill the beak section with golden brown line icing. Use the same icing to add tiny lines at the bottom, for feet.

- For the wing and tail feathers, add a row of scallop patterning, leave to dry, then add a second row, then a third. I used a 3-2-1 pattern.

- Use red line icing to add a wattle underneath the beak. For the comb, use the same icing to add a thickish section of red along the top of the head. Use a cocktail stick to tease the icing upwards. Do this a few times. As the icing starts to stiffen, the peaks will stay.

- Finish with a dot of black on white, for an eye.

Sheep

- Outline the biscuit with white line icing, then flood with white. Leave to dry.

- For the woolly curls, use white line icing to add spiral patterns. Start at one end of the sheep and add swirls around the outer edge of the biscuit, before filling in the middle. Don't do so many that the icing starts to run together.

- With black line icing, add tiny lines across the bottom of the feet, for toes and a black dot for a nose. Use white line icing to add a mouth and finish with a dot of black on white, for an eye.

Cow

- Outline the biscuit with white line icing, leaving a section for the udder, flood with white and leave to dry.

- Using pink line icing, outline and fill in the udder section.

- For the black patches, use black line icing to ice patch outlines in random spots on

the cow's body. Make the shapes completely freeform and have some bigger than others. Fill with the same icing. Fill in the second of the two ears and, while you have the black icing in your hand, add a line for a mouth. Shake the biscuit to smooth over and leave to dry.

- With white line icing, outline and fill hooves. Outline a tail, with small lines at the end.

- With pink line icing, add a pink dot for a nose and add some line detail on the udder.

- Finish by outlining the first ear with white line icing, and add a dot of black on white, for an eye.

Goose

- Outline the bird with white line icing, leaving sections for the beak and feet. Flood with white and leave to dry.

- Fill in the beak section with orange line icing. For the feet, use the same orange icing to add tiny lines. When the lines are dry, add a small blob of orange between each line, then drag with a cocktail stick to fill the gap. The goose now has webbed feet.
- Use white line icing to add feather detail on the wing and tail. Finish with a dot of black on white, for an eye.

The pig breeds

- The pigs collection shows what can happen when you get a biscuit idea in your head that won't go away. I just have to thank the British Pig Association; the photographs of all the pig breeds on their website formed the basis of the biscuit designs.

Large white

- Outline the biscuit with pink line icing, leaving a section for the tail, flood with pink and leave to dry.

- To add the line details, make sure your pink icing is fairly stiff, otherwise the tail and nose lines will not keep their shape. Add a small curl to the tail section and a round oval at the nose end. Add a curve for a second ear, outline the first ear and put a line underneath this ear, to offset it.
- Put two tiny dots inside the nose outline and add a pink smile.
- For the trotters, outline and fill with the same pink line icing. If you like, add a pink dot for a rosy cheek. For the eye, add a dot of black on white.

Tamworth

- Outline the biscuit with orange-brown line icing, leaving a section for the tail. Flood with orange-brown and leave to dry.
- To add the line details, use orange-brown line and decorate in the same way as for the large white, adding ear, nose, tail and trotters.
- If you like, add a pink dot for a rosy cheek. For the eye, add a dot of black on white.

Gloucestershire old spot

- Decorate the entire biscuit as for the large white and Tamworth, using pink icing.
- Then, with black line icing, add small black splodges randomly over the pig's body, and leave to dry.

Saddleback

- This pig is also decorated in the same way as the previous pigs, though, when initially outlining with black, leave a thick section clear down the middle of the pig. Outline and fill this section with white.
- Use black line icing to add the finishing line details, and add a dot of black on white, for an eye.

Berkshire

- Outline the biscuit with black line icing, leaving a section for the tail, nose and trotters. Flood with black and leave to dry.
- Use white line icing to fill in the nose section, and to outline and fill trotters.
- Add line details in exactly the same way as for the large white, using black line icing. If you like, add a pink dot for a rosy cheek. For the eye, add a dot of black on white.

DECORATING TIP: SPLODGY ANIMALS

Adding icing 'splodges' is an easy way to add colour and patterning to your biscuit animals.

Animal patches are not generally uniform or symmetrical, so adding splodges of different sizes and shapes to an animal will actually create exactly the effect you want. It is this randomness which makes the technique so easy.

Have a look at the three examples here: a pig, giraffe and cow. The pig's muddy splashes, the giraffe's brown patches and the Friesian cow's black patches all have wobbly edges and have not been placed in an even pattern.

Creating this effect is a simple matter of squishing some icing onto the biscuit and shaping it, if necessary with a cocktail stick, though these three examples each show a different variation on this basic technique. The pig's muddy splodges were added when the biscuit was completely finished. All I did was to add some blobs of brown line icing, and push it about a bit with the tip of the icing bag. I didn't even bother with the cocktail stick. For the giraffe, the patches were added while the golden brown flood icing was still wet. I used dark brown flood icing, simply because the patches are quite big and line icing would not be able to get the coverage.

With the cow, I used the outline and fill technique, simply because I wanted to give each splodge a curvy shape. So, I outlined each splodgy patch first, before filling it in and giving the biscuit a shake on the table top to smooth the surface.

All three techniques are quick and easy. And if you have added a splodge that doesn't look quite right, reassure yourself that there is probably an animal out there, somewhere, that has a splodge that exactly matches the one on your biscuit.

THE ANIMALS WENT IN TWO BY TWO...

If you have children who are into animals, then there is no limit when it comes to biscuits. Just think 'zoo' and you are away. The only possible restriction is getting hold of cutters but, and I can say this without checking, my collection of zoo animal cutters is my largest. I have chosen a few favourites here, and have given it a Noah's ark theme because, when I found the cutter online, I couldn't resist buying it. The final choice of animals to board the boat is yours.

The cutters
Ark
Giraffe
Penguin
Lion
Hippo
Bear
Camel
Tortoise
Elephant
Crocodile

The biscuits
Vanilla with wholemeal, or
chocolate

Icing – line
Light brown
Brick
*Made by adding a drop of brown
to burgundy.*
Sand
*Made by adding drops of yellow,
orange and brown to white icing.*
Sky blue
Black
White
Yellow or golden brown
*Made by adding a tiny drop of
brown to buttercup yellow.*
Dark brown
Orange
Black
White
Hippo grey
*Made by mixing a drop of purple
into grey icing.*
A selection of bright colours
for camel saddlecloths
Dark green
Ivory
Pink

Grey-blue
*Made by mixing drops of
delphinium blue, sky blue and the
tiniest dot of black.*

Icing – flood
Light brown
Brick
Sand
Black
White
Yellow or golden brown
Dark brown
Hippo grey
Grey-blue
Pale green
*I used avocado colour with a drop
of leaf green.*

The ark
- Outline the hull of the ark
  with light brown line icing,
  then flood.
- Outline the section for the
  roof with brick line icing,
  then flood. Do not worry
  about trying to outline a neat
  scallop along the bottom,
  just ice a straight line. The
  scallop detail can be added
  later.
- When dry, use sand line icing
  to outline the section in the
  middle, then flood.
- With brick line icing, outline
  a rectangular shape on the
  hull, for a door, and flood.

- In the middle section, use sky blue line icing to outline three square windows, and fill straight away with the same icing.

- When the biscuit is completely dry, add line details. Using sand line icing, outline the hull, and add four straight lines across, to mark the planks of wood. Do the same thing with the middle section. Outline with light brown and add horizontal straight lines, and also outline the window panes.

- Add four or five rows of scallop patterning across the roof, using brick line icing. Leave a few minutes between adding each row. Make sure you ice the patterning so that the tips of the curves touch the bottom of the curves, on the row above. Space the rows evenly and so that the bottom row is iced along the bottom edge. Then add three straight lines along the top and sides.

- Using brick line icing, ice line details around the door, and add two black dots for handles.

- For each dove, ice one largish white blob, using line icing, for a body then, while the icing is wet, ice a smaller second blob for the head. Use a cocktail stick to shape the dove, bringing the blobs of icing together and dragging upward at the back to make a tail. Repeat this process for the second dove and leave to dry.

- Add tiny beaks, using sand line icing, and neaten with a cocktail stick if needed.

- Add two small black lines to each, for feet, and give each a tiny black dot for an eye.

Giraffes

- Outline the biscuit, except for the tail, nose and ears, with yellow or golden brown line icing. Outline the tail, nose and ears with dark brown and fill straight away with the same icing.

- Flood the giraffe with icing to match the outline colour and, while wet, add splodges of dark brown flood icing. Leave to dry completely.

- Add three toes using dark brown line icing, doing the outside toes before the middle toes.

- Finish with a brown line smile and a dot of black on white, for an eye.

Penguins

- Outline the head and wings first, using black line icing. Make sure you outline only the top half of the wings. Flood with black and leave to dry.

- Outline the underside of the penguin's wings and down his sides, with white line icing. Outline two semi-circles along the bottom of the biscuit, for his feet. Before flooding, fill a section underneath his head with orange line icing. Flood the penguin's body with white, running the icing into the orange icing. With a cocktail stick, feather the orange into the white.

- With orange line icing, add a large orange spot on the side

of the penguin's head. With a cocktail stick, drag the spot so that it has a point at the bottom. Add an orange line for a mouth, dragging it to a point with a cocktail stick, if needed.

- Fill the space left for his feet, with black line icing. With a cocktail stick drag the icing while it is still wet, so it forms three distinct claws.

- Finish with an eye: a dot of black on white.

Hippos

- Outline the whole biscuit with hippo grey, then flood with the same colour flood icing and leave to dry.

- Add line detail, using hippo grey line icing. A tiny curl for a tail, a small curve for an ear

and a dot for a nostril. For the toes, ice the outside blobs first, then the middle ones.

- Finish with a dot of black on white for an eye.

Bears

- With dark brown line icing, outline the bear, leaving a section bare for the nose, tail and tummy. Flood with dark brown and leave to dry.

- With sand, or light brown, line icing, fill in the tummy section, nose section and add two curved lines to indicate the ears.

- Use black line icing to add three lines on each foot, for claws, and to add a nose and muzzle detail.

- Finish with two eyes: dots of black on white.

Camels

- Outline the body of the camel with sand line icing, leaving a section for saddlecloth, ear, toes and nose.

- Use dark brown line icing to fill in the ear and nose.

- With sand line icing, ice small, rough, scraggly lines around the knees, tail and neck of the camel. Run a cocktail stick through the icing if the lines start to run together.

- Add three toes using sand line icing, doing the outside toes before the middle toes.

- For the saddlecloth, use line icing to add a square shape in the gap left by the sand outlining and then, in a contrasting colour, add a second inner square. When

dry, ice straight lines across in a zig-zag fashion. Let the first set of lines dry before adding the second.

- Ice dots around the edge of the saddlecloth and add ragged knot ends, in a contrasting colour.

- Use dark brown line icing to add a smile, and add an eye with a dot of black on white.

Tortoises

- With dark brown line icing, outline the tortoise's shell. Within the shell, outline shell plates, roughly square in shape. Go over the lines again, to make them thick and high. This will make them stand out after the sections have been filled in. Leave to dry.

- Outline the remainder of the tortoise with sand or light brown line icing, flood and leave to dry.

- To finish the shell, fill in each plate section with dark green line icing, pushing it into the corners with a cocktail stick. While the icing is still wet, ice a line of ivory into each section. Drag through the ends of each line with a cocktail stick to make tapered semi-circle patterns. Leave to dry.

- Add sand or light brown line markings on the body. With ivory line icing, add three toes on each foot.

- For the tortoise's face, use brown line icing to give him a wiggly smile and a dot for a nose. With pink, add a rosy cheek, and finish with a dot of black on white, for an eye.

Elephants

- Outline the whole biscuit with grey-blue line icing, then flood.

- When the biscuit is dry, add line detail, with grey-blue line icing. On each foot, add the two outside blobs for toes and, when dry, add the middle toes. Add a tiny curl for a tail, a line at the tip of the trunk and a curve for an ear.

- For tusks, ice a thick line of white, using line icing. You may need to go back over the line a couple of times to get the right thickness. Use a cocktail stick to spread and thicken the tusk at the top.

Finish with a dot of black on white, for an eye.

Crocodiles

- Outline the crocodile in dark green. Be sure to leave a section for the mouth and underbelly, and outline the front and back legs, and the curves in the tail.

- When dry, flood with pale green. While the icing is still wet, add a pattern of small dots, using dark green line icing. Make the dots smaller as you go down the crocodile's body. Leave to dry.

- Add the claws, using white line icing. Do the two outside claws first, by icing blobs that

are then teased to a point with a cocktail stick. When dry, add the middle claw.

- For the teeth, add two rows of small dots, using white line icing. Then, with a cocktail stick, drag the dots so that each has a point. Don't crowd the mouth with too many teeth, otherwise you risk the teeth touching and running together.

- Finish your croc by adding two black dots for nostrils, a dot of black on white for an eye, and an arc of dark green line icing over the eye.

DESIGN TIP: TO FLOOD OR NOT TO FLOOD?

No, I am not making a biblical reference. The question concerns whether or not you want to flood the complete surface of your biscuit with icing or leave the biscuit as, biscuit, and just add some line details and features.

Have a look at the lions here. One has his body filled with a sandy beige colour while the second has, as his body, the biscuit base.

This is one reason why my vanilla with wholemeal recipe is my all-time favourite. It creates a biscuit with colour, and just a little bit of texture. Have another look at the biscuit lion. The golden colour of the biscuit with the flecks of wholemeal makes a perfect lion's coat. What has worked here for lions works with other biscuits as well. Practically any animal that has a brownish coat can be left uniced, or part uniced. I have decorated giraffes, kangaroos, bears and hedgehogs, along with others, this way, and they look great.

But the biggest advantage is the time saving. Not flooding a whole biscuit surface cuts out what is probably the most time-consuming decorating process. Even more time is saved if it means you don't have to make up icing of both line and flood consistency.

Also, if you are decorating biscuits for younger children, it may make you feel better giving them a biscuit which is not totally covered with icing. They will give you a smile and eat up the biscuit regardless.

Lions

- Outline the lion's body with sand line icing, leaving sections for the mane, toes and tail.
- Outline the mane section, using dark brown line icing, add a blob of dark brown for a nose and a second blob for the tail. Ice three lines on each foot, for claws.
- Flood the mane with dark brown. When dry, ice small lines to add hair detail. I used a mix of sand, light brown and dark brown lines. Use whatever colours you have, that are suitable.
- Finish with a line of brown for a smile, and a dot of black on white for an eye.

A FLOCK OF FUNKY FLAMINGOS

Someone once made the comment that my biscuits look like pottery – bisque-its, if you like. This thought stayed with me and, when I planned a batch of flamingos, for no reason other than I had just bought the cutter and really wanted to use it, I chose to ice them with earthy, pottery inspired colours. So instead of being an obvious pink, these flamingos are far funkier – modern, stylish and graphic. The thick layer of chocolate biscuit underneath makes the icing look like glaze on earthenware.

The cutters
Flamingo

The biscuits
Chocolate

Icing – line
Flamingo peach
See Decorating tip: Mixing new colours.
Dark brown
Pale pink
Light brown
Black
White

Icing – flood
Flamingo peach
Dark brown

- First, outline the body shape of the flamingo with flamingo peach line icing. Flood, then leave to dry completely.

- Outline the legs and feet in dark brown line icing. When dry, flood with dark brown.

- Fill in the small beak section with pale pink and leave to dry.

- Using dark brown line icing, add the shape for the flamingo's wing. I ice an approximate shape and then give it pointed tips by dragging a cocktail stick through the ends of the wings. Leave to dry.

- With black line icing, add a black tip to the pink beak then, while this icing is still wet, ice a black line to finish the beak.

- Using light brown line icing, add detail to the feet. Again, use a cocktail stick to neaten and to draw the icing to the edge of the bird's foot.

- Add an eye. A dot of white followed straight away with a small dot of black.

- A thin line of black line icing under the wing is the last detail. A cocktail stick will help to tease the ends of the line to tapered points.

DECORATING TIP: **MIXING NEW COLOURS**

Don't be limited in your colour choices by the names on your pots or bottles. Mixing new colours can make your finished biscuits that bit more original.

Just go slowly, adding one colour at a time, dot by dot, using the end of a cocktail stick. If you go too far, a drop or two of white will lighten up your icing to the point where you can start adding colour again. But don't keep dumping in random colours haphazardly just to see what happens, otherwise you will create icing that is more of a witch's brew – overloaded with colours and not tasting particularly nice.

When I designed my flamingos, I mixed a new colour for the bird's body. I didn't want pink, but 'earthenware'; something more orange or brown, but still with hints of coral or peach. So while I had a definite colour in mind, there was no one bottle of food colour to match. So I got mixing. I started off with terracotta colour, which was too orangey and bright. I then toned it down with a tiny drop of brown. To add the coral tones, I then added a good couple of drops of peach colour. At this point, while I had the right shade, it was too deep and dark. A couple of drops of white – perfect.

Number and letter biscuits. Fun, easy-to-decorate and versatile. I have often baked and decorated number biscuits for my daughter to take to her friends' birthday parties. We have tracked the passing of years in biscuits. Other options are spelling out the name of the birthday girl or boy in letters, or making simple messages.

The cutters
Letters
Numbers

The biscuits
Vanilla with wholemeal, or chocolate

Icing – line
Pink
White
Black
Aqua
Cornflower blue
Dark brown
Yellow
Purple

Icing – flood
Pink
White
Aqua
Cornflower blue
Yellow
Purple

Note on colours and shapes
The colours and designs shown here can be adapted for any numbers or letters.

Optional glitter and sprinkles
Pink glitter
Gold glitter
Pink, girly sprinkles
White chocolate stars

Happy birthday
- Outline the letters with pink and cornflower blue line icing. I alternated colours.
- Flood one letter at a time, with the matching colour flood icing. While the flood icing is still wet, add spots of random size in the contrasting flood colour. Add a few large spots first, then a few more medium spots, then fill any obvious gaps with very small dots. Leave to dry.

Balloons

- In your chosen colour (I used pink and cornflower blue to match the 'happy birthday' biscuits), outline then flood. While the flood icing is still wet, add a dot of white flood icing to the top right of the balloon. While still wet, drag two or three times through the dot with a cocktail stick.

- When completely dry, ice a wiggly line near the base, to indicate where the balloon has been tied.

Pink 2 with brown stitching

- Outline with pale pink, flood, then leave to dry.

- With dark brown line icing, add small lines all around the edge of the biscuit, to look like stitching.

Purple 5

- Outline with purple line icing, then flood. While the flood icing is still wet, add a pattern of tiny dots over the biscuits, with white line icing.

Jewel encrusted 6

- These biscuits are extremely easy to do. I like to describe them as 'jewel encrusted'.

- With pink line icing, squeeze squiggles over the biscuit. You don't need to cover the whole surface, just squiggle over enough wiggly lines for the sprinkles to stick to.

- For the 'jewels', I like to mix up a selection of pink, girly sprinkles on a plate. I then gently push the biscuit into the mix, while the icing is wet, so the sprinkles stick.

- Then, if you like, add some glitter over the top of the sprinkles, to really enhance the sparkly finish.

9 with stars

- These are perfect for a boy's birthday.

- Outline with aqua, and flood with the same colour.

- While the icing is still wet, gently push five or six white chocolate stars into the icing, then leave to dry.

Black and white 50

- These were made for a couple's 50th birthday.

- Outline the numbers with white line icing, flood and leave to dry.

- Add swirls, using black line icing. Starting and finishing each swirl with a dot will ensure they look neat. Add dots, decreasing in size, on either side of each swirl.

Golden 50

- These are perfect for a wedding anniversary.

- Outline the numbers with yellow line icing, then flood.

- While the icing is still wet, add a generous amount of gold glitter, so the biscuits are fully coated. Brush off the excess glitter when dry.

CRETACEOUS COOKIES

I had originally called this collection 'Jurassic park' but a friend pointed out that most of the dinosaurs here were from the Cretaceous period. Then I decided I liked the sound of 'Cretaceous cookies' better, anyway. But that is where scientific accuracy starts and ends. I am sure palaeontologists have made great progress in pinpointing many dinosaurs' exact features and colours, but these are biscuits, not museum pieces, so these dinos are cartoonish in shape, fun and friendly – even the tyrannosaurus doesn't look that scary – and oh so brightly coloured.

The cutters
A selection of dinosaurs

The biscuits
Chocolate

Icing – line
Dark brown
Black
White
Aqua

Icing – flood
A selection of bright colours
I used aqua, purple, yellow, green and orange.

Note on colours
For this collection, I created the designs using a mix of these colours, but give decorating instructions for only one example of each design. You can mix up the colours as you wish.

Brontosaurus

- Outline with dark brown line icing. When dry, flood with green. While the flood icing is still wet, add dots of purple flood icing. Do a few large dots, then add some more medium dots, then finish with very small dots, wherever there are obvious gaps on the body. Leave to dry completely.

- Add line detail with dark brown. Add two blobs for outer toes on each foot and, when dry, fill in with the middle toe. Give him a smiley mouth and add a tiny dot for a nose.

- Finish with a dot of black on white, for an eye.

Triceratops

- Outline the body with dark brown line icing, leaving sections for the horns. Include a line to indicate the frill around the neck. Then outline and fill the horns.

- When dry, flood with aqua. While the flood icing is still

wet, add thick lines of yellow flood icing down the body. Use a cocktail stick to taper each line to a point.

- Add line detail with dark brown. Add three lines on each foot, for claws. Give him a smiley mouth and add a tiny dot for a nose. Ice tiny dots down the frill section.

- Finish with a dot of black on white, for an eye.

Tyrannosaurus rex
- Outline the body with dark brown line icing, including an outline to mark out the back leg. Do not outline right to the edge of the mouth: leave sections uniced, for teeth.

- For the spots, use the same dark brown to ice a number of round circles, of various sizes.

- When dry, fill in the circles with aqua icing. Use flood icing for the larger circles and line icing for the smaller circles.

- Flood the remainder of the body with yellow flood icing. Use a cocktail stick to push icing around the aqua spots. Give the biscuit a good shake to smooth over the icing.

- When dry, use dark brown to add line detail: three lines on each foot and hand, for claws, and a tiny dot for a nose.

- For his teeth, ice two rows of small white dots along the inside of his mouth. While the icing is still wet, tease each dot to a point, using a cocktail stick.

- Finish with a dot of black on white, for an eye.

Stegosaurus

- Create the plates along the dinosaur's back first. With dark brown line icing, outline diamond shapes, but with a flat bottom. Fill with the same icing and leave to dry.

- Then outline the body, but ice the line lower over the back, so that the plates stand out. Include lines to indicate the front and back legs.

- Flood with purple icing. While the icing is still wet, add dots of yellow flood icing, in the same way as for the brontosaurus. Leave to dry completely.

- Use dark brown line icing to give the stegosaurus toes, a smile and a dot for a nose.

- Finish with a dot of black on white, for an eye.

DESIGN TIP: **ALL SORTS OF SPOTS**

Spots turn up all the time in this book. They are easy to do, but always look striking.

The dinosaurs were no exception: they just had to be spotty. Okay, the triceratops is stripy, but he isn't my favourite (you are allowed to have favourite dinosaurs).

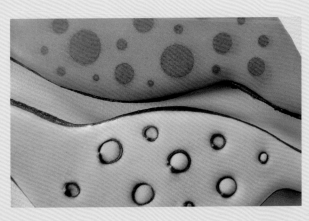

What I wanted, however, was spots with a difference. I love adding spots straight onto flood icing, as you get a nice flat finish, but the drawback can be a slight fluffiness to the edge of the spot. I wanted my dinosaur spots to really stand out, so decided to try icing round circles before filling them in. Plus, I wanted to create a slightly textured finish, thinking that a slight bumpiness – a lunar landscape skin – might look a bit more reptilian.

I used dark brown line icing for all the outlining because it was a great match with the chocolate biscuit base, and iced seven or eight circles of random sizes before filling them in.

The finished effect was textured and uneven, just what I wanted, but the drawback was that it was quite time consuming and fiddly. Some circles were not very round and had to be scraped off the biscuit and re-done. It was also quite slow and finicky pushing the flood icing for the body all around the circles.

I did some of the usual spots straight onto the wet icing to compare. They also looked great (though I still prefer my bumpy-skinned dinosaurs). So, the tip is to build up the decorating techniques in your repertoire, even for things as simple as spots. Then, depending on your time and inclination, you will have more options available to you when planning your biscuit designs.

BOYS' CLASSIC TOYS

This is the collection for the tree-climbing, fort-building, frog-catching boys out there. Admittedly, these seem like somewhat nostalgic pastimes, though I think we grown-ups still hang on to the idea that our children enjoy the same simple games and toys that we did, before the onslaught of all things electronic and excessively branded. So, be charmed by the classic toys shown here. Batteries not needed.

The cutters
Yacht
Rocketship
Scots Guard
London taxi
Fighter plane

The biscuits
Vanilla with wholemeal

Icing – line
Blue
Red
Brown
Navy blue
Gold
Pink
Skintone
Made by adding drops of pink and brown to ivory, then lightening with white.
Grey
Yellow
White
Black

Icing – flood
Blue
Red
Navy blue
Grey
Yellow
White
Black

Optional sprinkles
White chocolate stars

Yacht
- Outline the hull section with blue line icing, flood with blue, and leave to dry.
- When dry, use brown line icing to add a thick vertical line, for a mast. Also add a horizontal line and dots along the hull. Leave to dry.
- Use white line icing to outline two sails and flood with white. When dry, use red line icing to outline and then fill two red bands across the sail.
- Finish by adding a small red triangle at the top of the mast, for a flag.

Rocketship
- Outline the whole rocketship, with the exception of the tailfins, with blue line icing, flood, then leave to dry completely.
- Outline the top and bottom sections with white line icing, then flood with white. Use flood icing to add a large dot in the centre. Leave to dry completely.
- Use white line icing to add dots, for rivets, around the edges of the white sections.
- Outline the tailfin sections with red line icing, and add a thick line down the bottom centre, for a third fin. Flood with red, then leave to dry.

Scots Guard
- Outline the bearskin section with black line icing, then flood with black.
- With red line icing, outline the tunic section, flood and leave to dry.
- Use navy blue line icing to outline the trousers, flood, then leave to dry.

- Line icing can be used for the remainder of the decorating.

- For the face and hands, outline and fill with skintone. Leave the face and hands to dry before adding dots for ears and thumbs, and a dot in the middle of the face for a nose.

- Outline and fill the boots with black.

- With navy, outline and fill cuffs, and add a line down the centre of the trousers.

- Use red to add lines to indicate the sleeves, and stripes down either side of the legs.

- With white, add a line down the centre of the jacket, to represent the piping. Outline and fill a thick band across the jacket's middle, for a belt. For the cuff detail, ice a thick white band at the bottom of each sleeve. Then, with a cocktail stick, drag through the icing to create three points on each. Leave to dry.

- Add gold, or yellow, dots for buttons on the white cuffs and down the centre of the jacket. Add a dot in the centre of the belt, with two lines either side, for a buckle.

- Finish with a face. A pink smile, two pink rosy cheeks, dots of black on white for eyes, and two small black eyebrows.

London taxi

- With black line icing, outline the outside of the biscuit, leaving the bottom sections uniced, but including the wheels. Flood with black and leave to dry.

- With grey line icing, outline and fill the bumper and running boards along the bottom of the biscuit. At the same time, add two large round dots, for wheel hubs, and outline three windows. Add a vertical line at the front, for a radiator, and a dot at the top of this line, for a headlight.

- Flood the windows with white. Add black line details: door outlines, handles, tyres.

- To finish, add dots of red and black at the taxi's rear, for taillights.

British fighter plane

- Outline the plane's fuselage section with grey line icing. Add more outlines for the wings and tail fins. Flood with grey and leave to dry.

- For the engine cowling, outline with grey line icing and, when dry, flood with navy blue.

- For the cockpit canopy, use white line icing to add a largish oval blob to the centre of the fuselage. Shape it with a cocktail stick. When it is dry, circle around it with grey line icing and add horizontal and vertical lines to create a grid pattern.

- With the same grey icing, add a tailfin at the end of the fuselage.

- Add a red line, for a propeller hub. When this is dry, add two small grey lines, for propeller blades

- Finish the plane by adding roundels to the wings and tailfins. Add round blobs of navy blue flood icing. Straight away add a smaller round blob of white flood icing, straight on top of the navy. Then immediately dot the top with red line icing. Give the biscuit a shake to get the icing to settle.

US fighter plane

- The yellow and red American plane is decorated in much the same way as the British plane. The main variation is the colours chosen.

- I also iced the fuselage and cowling slightly differently. I first outlined and flooded the red fuselage, then outlined and filled the grey cowling separately, rather than over the top of the fuselage section, as I did with the British plane. But it really does not matter which way you do it.

- For the US roundels on the wing, add a blob of navy blue flood icing, then stick on a white chocolate star. On top of the star, add a dot of red line icing. The stars are too big for the tailfin roundels. For these, add a round blob of navy blue flood icing, then wait for it to dry completely. Add a blob of white line icing, and use a cocktail stick to drag the edges of the blob to make the star's points. When dry, top with a tiny dot of red line icing.

THE BISCUIT LABORATORY

This collection was a biscuit experiment that produced fantastic results. Bubbly potions bright enough to make your eyes water. Be reassured though, they are perfectly safe for consumption, and might just taste of vanilla. Perfect for all the mad scientists out there.

The cutters
Test tube
Beaker
Round-bottomed flask
Flat-bottomed flask
These 'cutters' were home-made (see Baking tip, opposite).

The biscuits
Vanilla with wholemeal

Icing – line and flood
Glassy white
Made by mixing tiny specks of black and cornflower blue with a lot of white.
Electric purple
Electric blue
Electric pink
Electric green
The colours used for this collection come from a very specific colour range: 'Electric'. Other colours can be used, but you won't get the same neon glow.

Optional glitter
Pink, purple, green and blue

Decorating steps

- The decorating steps outlined here apply for all the shapes in the collection.

- With line icing in your chosen colour, outline the bottom two-thirds of the biscuit, flood with the corresponding flood icing, then leave to dry completely.

- Outline the top part of the biscuit with glassy white line icing, flood, then leave to dry.

- For the bubbles, use flood icing. Invert the bottle and add blobs of colour along the left side of the biscuit. A biggish squeeze will give you a big dot, just dabbing the tip of the nozzle will give you a tiny dot. Aim for about 10 or so dots, with a mix of sizes, but concentrate the bigger dots at the bottom and the smallest dots at the top. When adding the bigger dots, use the tip of the nozzle or a cocktail stick to move the icing around gently in a circular motion, which will spread and flatten the dots a little.

- Apply glitter, if using, straight away while the dots are wet. Leave to dry before brushing off the excess.

- Add line detail with glassy white icing. Add a lozenge-shape at the very top, to represent the lip and, inside this shape, ice a tiny dash at the left. Ice a series of dashed lines down the right-hand size to indicate millimetres. A curved line extending about three-quarters across the middle of the biscuit will give the biscuit a rounded appearance. Lastly, if the shape is the test tube or round-bottomed flask, add a small curved line at the bottom left.

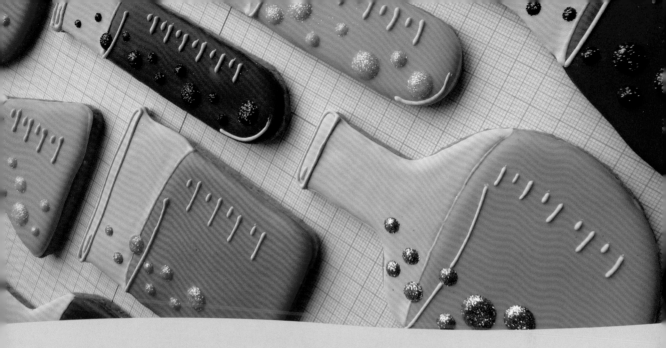

BAKING TIP: CREATING YOUR OWN 'CUTTERS'

When the call came in for some science-themed biscuits for a birthday party, my first instinct was to try to persuade the mother to go for another collection. The reason was that I just didn't have any appropriate cutters.

It was my husband who suggested cutting plastic templates. He sketched some designs, and then he used scissors to cut the shapes from a thin piece of flexible plastic pulled from the depths of his toolshed.

To cut out the biscuits, I rolled out the dough onto my reusable baking parchment, so that I could cut around the templates without having to worry about scratching my work surface. My smallest vegetable knife proved to be best for the job.

Once baked, the biscuits looked great. When I had finished decorating them, I knew the extra effort had been worth it. They looked fantastic and the family loved them.

Having the templates made from plastic meant that I could wash them up and keep them. For this reason, I recommend seeking out plastic of some sort if you want to attempt your own. Overhead transparencies work well, as does the stiff plastic that is used for the covers of display books – the sort used for school projects.

Stiff cardboard is fine, so long as you don't want to keep your template or don't plan on making too many biscuits. With lots of cutting around it, the template edges can get nicked or crumpled, and you need to flour it to stop it sticking to the dough.

OUT OF THE TOYBOX

A house with two daughters means piles of soft toy animals are in residence, making it inevitable that a soft toy biscuit collection would materialise at some point. Teddy bears are an obvious choice, but don't stop there. Just about any animal shape, decorated with a bright colour and with stitches added, becomes a soft, cuddly toy. And I don't mean the plush, fluffy things that are available commercially but the more old-fashioned ones; the fabric ones sewn together with love by aunts and grandmothers, and bought at craft fairs.

The cutters
Teddy bear
Rabbit
Koala
Pig
Elephant

The biscuits
Vanilla with wholemeal

Icing – line
Light brown
Made by mixing brown, white and dots of yellow.
Yellow
Aqua
Dark grey
Light grey
Pink
Purple
Black
White
Dark brown

Icing – flood
Light brown
Yellow
Aqua
Dark grey
Light grey

Pink
Purple
If you are making these biscuits for a child, it makes sense to ask what their preferred colours are.

Teddy bear
- Outline the whole biscuit with light brown line icing, then flood and leave to dry.
- Add the paws by making four oval-ish blobs at the end of the arms and legs with dark brown line icing, and adding three dots for toes.

- Add the stitching, by icing on small lines of dark brown line icing. Start with the head first, then add the ear stitching, the body and finish by stitching the arms and legs.
- Add two pink dots inside the ears. For his face, add a dot of dark brown line icing and extend two lines from the dot to make two curves. Use a cocktail stick to make the dot into a more triangular shape.
- For his tie, use any bright-coloured line icing. Add a dot, then add triangle shapes either side. Shape the wet icing with a cocktail stick.
- Finish by adding a dot of black on white, for an eye.

Rabbit
- Outline the biscuit with yellow line icing, leaving a small section for the tail. Flood with yellow. While the

- Add a tiny dark brown dot for a nose, and two curves underneath the dot, for a mouth.
- Finish the rabbit by adding two dots of black on white, for eyes.

- Use black line icing to add an oval blob for a nose. When this is dry, add a tiny line of pink underneath, for a mouth, and two dots of black on white, for eyes.

icing is still wet, add dots of aqua flood icing. Add the dots to the rabbit's body only, in an even pattern.

- When dry, fill in the tail section with aqua line icing and two dots of yellow flood icing. Leave to dry completely.
- Add two thickish lines of aqua line icing, for the inner ears.
- Then add the dark brown stitching. Do the tail first, then continue up around the back, and down the middle of the ears. Continue in a curve to mark the face. Keep going down the front, then curve up to indicate a front paw. Go back to the tail, stitch along and add curves for the back leg. Then stitch the last section along the bottom.

Koala

- With light grey line icing, outline a round section for the koala's head. Flood with light grey icing and leave to dry.
- Outline a round section for the body, with dark grey icing, and flood.
- When dry, use black line icing to fill in the two ears and the bottom paw. Use light grey line icing to fill in the upper paw.
- When dry, add stitching, with black line icing. Stitch the head first, then the round body, then the paws and ears.

Muddy piggy

- Outline the biscuit with pale pink line icing, then flood with pink and leave to dry.
- Add muddy splodges, with dark brown line icing. Simply push on a generous blob of icing, then use a cocktail stick to spread the blotch a bit. Aim for a random effect.
- Add the stitching, with dark brown line icing. Stitch around the outside of the pig, then add stitching for the two legs.
- Use pink line icing to add a smiley mouth, and line details to indicate the nose and ear. Lastly, add a dot of black on white, for an eye.

Elephant

- Outline the biscuit with pale pink line icing, then flood. While the icing is still wet, add dots of purple flood icing, in an even pattern, and leave to dry.

- Add a purple tusk using line icing, and use a cocktail stick to drag the end to a point. Add a tiny line of purple across the end of the trunk.

- Add the stitching. With dark brown line icing, start with the ear, stitching a curve around and up the head, around the trunk and around the body and legs, to finish along the elephant's back. Add extra stitching around the tail.

- Finish with a dot of black on white, for an eye.

DESIGN TIP: INSPIRED BY CHILDREN

When I was delivering this very batch of biscuits to a café, a woman asked me "Are you the person who designs these biscuits?" The bit that flattered me was her choice of words: design. No one had explicitly called me a 'biscuit designer' before. What a job description.

This collection, more than any other, shows the myriad of sources that can inspire you when designing your biscuits. While it is true that I had 'soft toys' as an idea in my head for some time, they became a reality when a mother asked me to make rabbit biscuits for her daughter's fourth birthday.

I didn't want to do plain brown rabbits for a party and besides, the birthday-girl-to-be had requested blue. The inspiration then came from one of my own toddler daughter's outfits. The elephants running around the bottom of the top and trousers were the same simple shape as biscuit elephants. So I borrowed a few of the elements: the brown stitching and the spots, and created the blue rabbits.

From there, it was very easy to take this basic stitching technique and create a whole range of soft toy biscuits, in lots of colours.

I have found that having children provides no end of design inspiration. I have been inspired by book illustrations, looked to their clothes for colour ideas and even consulted their plastic farm and jungle animals when designing and decorating.

So the tip here is simple: for design ideas, just look all around you, and don't be afraid to raid your children's wardrobe!

FOR THE FAIRY PRINCESSES

All little girls are fairy princesses. And so their loving mums organise appropriately themed birthday parties for them, complete with fairy princess table settings, party bags and so on. What follows is the flutter of wings, whereby the guests descend, all dressed in their pinkest, sparkliest fairy dresses, accessorised with tiaras and wands. This biscuit collection was designed to complement such attire: I deliberately went for an overload of pink and glitter to match the excess of the dress-up fairy frocks. And let me tell you, there is nothing like these biscuits to light up the fairy princesses' faces. 'Ooohs' and 'aaahs' all round. This particular batch was made for a five-year-old's birthday party. The perfect age, I think.

The cutters
Wand
Goblin, gnome or elf
Tiara
There are many different cutters available that are crown and tiara shaped. Whichever you choose, just adapt the design to fit.

The biscuits
Vanilla with wholemeal

Icing – line
White
Lemon
Made by whitening yellow icing.
Pale pink
Fuchsia
Purple
Lilac
Made by whitening purple icing.
Yellow
Dark green
Orange
Black
Dark green
Avocado green

Icing – flood
Lemon
Lilac
Pale pink
Avocado green
Purple
When describing the decorating steps, I refer to the colours used on these particular examples, however, the colours are interchangeable.

Glitter
I think this is the one collection where glitter is not optional, but mandatory.
I used white, pastel pink, pastel lilac, jewel lavender, jewel fuchsia, pastel green, gold and jewel ocean spray.
As this collection involves a lot of glittering, I have only instructed to leave the glitter to dry before brushing off the excess, in the first instance. Naturally, assume that this is carried out whenever glitter is applied.

Pink on lemon tiara
- Outline the whole tiara with lemon line icing, flood, then leave to dry.

- With pale pink line icing, outline the tiara pattern onto the flooded biscuit. Outline five peaks, with a deep curve between each peak, and room for jewels on top of the peaks and along the bottom. Flood with pale pink and add pastel pink glitter, leave to dry and then brush off the excess.

- Using lilac line icing, add dots at the top of the four peaks, five evenly spaced dots along the bottom, and four dots at the top of the middle peak, to make a flower. Add pastel lilac glitter while still wet.

- Add a dot of pink in the middle of the flower, using line icing, and a series of smaller pink dots in between the dots along the bottom.

- Link up the pink tiara peaks with four or five dots of fuchsia line icing.

middle, fill in straight away with the same icing, then add jewel fuchsia glitter.

- Add the pearls. With white line icing, add five large round pearls at the top of the tiara, five evenly spaced large pearls at the bottom, then lines of smaller pearls, with four to a strand. Add two of these smaller pearls between the top pearl and the pink heart. Make sure the pearls do not touch, are lined up evenly, and work quickly enough so that the icing remains wet enough for the white glitter, which you should add liberally as soon as you have finished the last pearl.

- With lilac line icing, add two strands of pearls between the white strands, with four to a strand. Line up the pearls with the white pearls and make the top pearl the biggest. Apply pastel lilac glitter.

- Using pale pink line icing, ice four medium dots between the large pearls at the bottom, and a series of small dots between each pearl, to link them up.

- Lastly, add a curve of fuchsia line icing around the top of each tiara peak, and cover with fuchsia glitter.

Pearls on lemon tiara

- Outline with lemon line icing, flood, then leave to dry.

- Start the detailing with the pearl flowers. At each tiara peak, add three balls of white line icing, being careful to make sure they don't touch. Cover with white glitter.

- Add a big fuchsia jewel at the very top and five evenly spaced, medium-sized fuchsia jewels, along the bottom. Cover with jewel fuchsia glitter.

- Using purple line icing, ice a scallop pattern, with deep curves, to link up the five pearl flowers. Add a second scallop pattern underneath the first. Apply jewel lavender glitter.

- Finish with fuchsia line details. Add a curved line underneath the purple scallop pattern, medium dots

Pearls on lilac tiara

- Outline with lilac line icing, flood, then leave to dry.

- With fuchsia line icing, outline a heart shape in the

between the fuchsia jewels at the bottom, and a series of very small dots all around the sides and top of the tiara.

Golden crown

- This is my interpretation of tiara cutter as crown. This is an option to give to boy party guests, or any girls who are rebelling against pink far earlier than you would expect.
- Outline with lilac line icing, flood and then leave to dry.
- With yellow line icing, carefully ice five small diamond shapes along the top of the crown, using a cocktail stick, if needed, to neaten the points. Add gold or pastel yellow glitter.
- Using lilac line icing, ice five lines of medium-sized dots downward from each gold jewel. Space them evenly and make them the same size. Cover with pastel lilac glitter.
- With dark green line icing, outline a large emerald at the

centre top of the crown, and fill straight away with the same icing. Use a cocktail stick to neaten and sharpen the points. Cover with jewel ocean spray glitter, or any dark green glitter.

- Outline around the crown, using yellow line icing. Ice deep down around the lines of purple dots, to create the crown shape.
- Lastly, use purple line icing to add a line along the bottom, and tiny dots at the points of the jewels.

Wand

- With yellow line icing, outline around the star shape at the top of the wand, then fill with the same icing.
- For the stem of the wand, outline with the same yellow, then fill straight away with the same line icing. Leave to dry.
- With fuchsia line icing, outline a star shape in the middle of the wand and fill with the same icing, shaping with a cocktail stick if needed. Put a small fuchsia

dot at the end of each star point, then cover with jewel fuchsia glitter.

- The wands are as adaptable as the tiaras when it comes to colour choice and design. You might also want to add some silver or gold dragees as part of the decoration.

Goblin

- What is this creature doing here? If there is a boy at the party who thinks a crown is too girly, or a younger brother who also demands a biscuit, well, they get to be goblins.
- With avocado green line icing, outline a shape for the goblin's face, giving him a pointy chin and pointy ears. Flood and leave to dry.
- Outline the goblin's clothes and hat with purple line

icing, leaving a section clear for his socks. Flood with purple and leave to dry.

- Add two spots of white line icing, for eyes. Use a cocktail stick to shape the eyes to a slight diamond shape. Add two dots of black for pupils. Use orange line icing to give him a cheeky smile and pink line icing for rosy cheeks. With dark green line icing, ice around the goblin's face, to emphasise the pointy chin and

ears. Add extra line detail for the ears, and give him pointy eyebrows and a pointy nose.

- Use orange line icing to outline the clothing. Put stripes across his hat and an orange bobble at the top. Carefully ice lines to indicate sleeves. Using the same orange, fill in his socks.

- When dry, add two medium-sized dots of avocado green line icing at the end of his sleeves, for hands, and two

smaller dots above, for thumbs.

- When dry, outline a square shape with yellow line icing, then fill with the same colour. Cover with gold glitter, to make a lantern. When the glitter is dry and you have shaken off the excess, use black line icing to ice panes on the lantern, and a small circle on top.

- Lastly, use white line icing to add stripes to the goblin's socks.

DESIGN TIP: SKETCHING YOUR IDEAS

I have to admit to being excited about doing the tiara biscuits. The bit I was really looking forward to was experimenting with design. And using all that glitter.

With a cutter like this, where I knew I could, and would, go mad with jewels, swirls and pearls and what not, I knew it was important to plan the design. For a

complete design. You need to plan out the extra details that will go with these swirls and think about what colours you want. You also run the risk that, while an idea can form in your head, it just might not materialise the way you want it on the biscuit.

For this collection, planning before decorating also meant

biscuit where anything goes in terms of colour and design, the planning is more important than with a more logical biscuit, such as an animal shape. This is because, even if you have an idea in mind, just going straight ahead with the icing is guaranteed not to work. While you may have an idea for a tiara with lots of pink swirls, for example, that isn't the

that I could develop different designs, but ones that could still make use of the same colour palette.

So, what I did was to draw around the cutter a number of times, and draw up a number of designs. As I did this, even more ideas for design elements and colours came into my head. I then picked my four favourites, made up the colours, and I was away.

A WOODLAND WALK

This is one of my most-requested collections. My reasoning is that the lovely autumn colours of the animals harmonise so well. It is also a collection with a very 'English' feel, a touch *Animals of Farthing Wood*. Or maybe it is because the hedgehogs are simply cute and the mushrooms are magical.

The cutters
Squirrel
Swan
Mushroom
Fox
Hedgehog
Deer

The biscuits
Vanilla with wholemeal

Icing – line
Grey
Red-brown
Made by adding orange or terracotta colour to brown icing.
Dark brown
Beige
Made by mixing white with a small amount of brown.
Light brown
Red
Green
Black
White

Icing – flood
Grey
Red-brown
Dark brown
Light brown
Red
White

Optional glitter
A bright green

Swan
- Outline the swan with white line icing, leaving a section for the beak. Flood with white and leave to dry.
- With red line icing, fill in the beak section and leave to dry.
- With white line icing, ice curve patterns on the body to represent wings and tail feathers.
- Finish by filling in a small black section between head and beak, and adding a sharp black dot, for an eye.

Squirrel
- These are the steps to decorate a grey squirrel. If you would like to decorate a red squirrel, just use red-brown icing instead of grey.
- Outline the squirrel with grey line icing, leaving sections uniced under the chin and for the stomach. Flood with grey.
- When dry, use white line icing to fill in the sections under the chin and for the stomach, and leave to dry. For the tail, ice a series of six or seven lines, the first black and the rest grey. Start at the top and finish with the last, smallest line underneath.
- Add a dot of grey line icing, for a nose. Use grey line icing to add small lines, for claws. Use the same icing to outline the ear tips and to add a nose. Extend a line from the nose to make a mouth.
- Finish with an eye: a dot of black on white.

Mushroom

- Outline the mushroom cap first, with red line icing. Leave the stalk and a thin section underside the cap.

- Flood the cap with red and, while the icing is still wet, add dots of white flood icing. Add the biggest dots first, then the medium-sized dots, then put four or five small dots in any gaps that are left, to create a random pattern. Leave to dry.

- Outline the remainder of the mushroom with white line icing, then flood with white and leave to dry.

- If you would like grass at the base of your mushroom, use green line icing to add a thick section of icing at the base. Use a cocktail stick to drag the wet icing upwards, to create blades of grass. Add green glitter, if you like.

Fox

- Outline the fox with red-brown line icing, leaving sections at the end of his tail, under his chin and for his underbelly. Flood with red-brown and leave to dry.

- Use white line icing to fill in the remaining sections.

- With dark brown line icing, add three lines to each foot

for claws, and outline the ear tips. Add a dot for a nose and extend a line from the dot to make a smile.

- For the fur detail on the tail, use line icing. Ice small lines here and there over the tail, being careful not to add too many in case the lines start to run together.

- Finish by adding two eyes: dots of black on white.

Hedgehog

- Outline the hedgehog's spiny section, with dark brown line icing. Leave the section along the bottom and a section for the face. Flood with dark brown and leave to dry.

- Outline the remaining section with beige line icing, then fill with the same icing and leave to dry.

- For the hedgehog's spines, choose two or three line colours. I used a brown and black. Add small lines, one colour at a time, evenly over the hedgehog.

- Use black line icing to add three tiny claws on each foot, a tiny nose and a small smile.

- Finish with a dot of black on white for an eye.

Fallow deer

- With light brown line icing, outline the deer's body, leaving a section for a tail, chest, underbelly, antler and feet.

- Flood with light brown. While the icing is still wet, add a series of small white dots on the body and back, using white line icing. Leave to dry.

- Fill in the chest and underbelly sections with white line icing. Do the same with the feet, leaving a section free at the bottom for hooves. Fill in the tail section with black line icing and leave to dry.

- For the antlers, use white line icing to outline the shape, then fill with the same icing and shake to smooth over. Use the same icing to fill a small inverted v-section on the tail.

- With black line icing, outline hoof shapes at the bottom of the legs and fill with the same icing.

- Go over the ear with light brown line icing, so that it stands out. Add a black dot of line icing for a nose.

- Add a dot of black on white, for an eye. Add white line detail inside the ear outline and finish by giving the deer a smile and an eyebrow, using light brown line icing.

icing more. Again, leave to dry before adding a few more. Keep going like this, until the broom is filled in. Once dry, ice three lines across the sticks with orange line icing. With the same orange, or brown, fill in the section underneath her hand, for the broomstick.

- For her hair, ice straggly black lines, as for the standing witch, leaving the first lot of lines to dry before adding more.

- Add an outline onto her robe, with black line icing, to define the shape of her sleeve. Leave to dry.

- Using line icing, add coloured lines to the end of her sleeve, the edge of her robe, and for her hat band. When dry, ice a small square of yellow on her hat band,

and add gold glitter to it, to create a buckle.

- Lastly, use black line icing to give her face a smile, and ice a small black dot on a white dot for her eye. If you want the witch to be warty, add a couple of brown dots to her face.

Spider's web

- Outline the outside of the web with black line icing. If you are using a round biscuit, put eight tiny dots at even intervals around the edge of the biscuit. Then connect these dots with curvy lines, to create a web outline.

- Flood with black. While the icing is still wet, add circles of colour, using line icing. For each web, I chose two colours. This one has white and orange. Carefully ice a circle of orange, then white, then orange, then white, starting at the outside and working in.

- Working quickly, use a cocktail stick to drag lines in the icing, from the middle out to each point. Wipe the cocktail stick clean after each drag, to avoid unwanted colour spots on your black web. When you are icing your initial colour circles on the web, it makes sense to start and finish each line in line with a point of the web. That way, if your icing is a bit untidy where the circles join up, then any flaws can be hidden by the drag of the cocktail stick. Leave to dry completely.

- For the spider, ice a largish blob of colour for his body. When I say largish, I mean of sufficient size to cover the very middle of the web, which may be a little untidy from all the cocktail stick drags. Leave to dry before adding a smaller blob for his head. Add two lines on either side of this body for legs and leave to dry before adding two more, between the first two. You need to leave time for the body parts and legs to dry before adding more, otherwise the icing will simply run together.

- Finish off the spider by adding two small black dots on top of two white dots, for eyes.

Tombstone

- Outline the whole tombstone with grey line icing, and then flood with grey.

- Add black line icing, to outline the tombstone and show the different sections. Use the same icing to write the letters 'RIP' in the centre. Leave to dry.

- With grey line icing, ice some cracks over the front of the tombstone.

- For the grass at the bottom, I used the same green icing and glitter as for the cauldron brew. Ice a thick section of green along the bottom, then use a cocktail stick to drag sections upward, to create tufts of grass. Sprinkle over green glitter, if you like.

DECORATING TIP: BLACK IS BLACK

Most cake and biscuit decorators know that getting a good, strong black colour can be tricky. It is easily the most difficult colour to achieve. Red and brown are my runners up.

Be careful how much colour you add. Adding black colour to your royal icing will seem to create nothing more than a dark grey colour. You may need to add more black colour to get a stronger shade, but it is important to remember that when icing dries, it dries a slightly darker shade than when it is wet. So, please don't pile in loads of black food colour in a desperate attempt to get your icing really, really black. Once you get to a dark charcoal-ish shade, stop. A very slight greyness to your black icing will disappear once it has dried.

Besides, if you are using black line as well as black flood icing, you can use black's stubbornness to your advantage. I think you need a really strong black for line detail, but for these Hallowe'en biscuits, I consciously made the black flood icing a touch lighter. Have a look at the close up of the bat – the slightly lighter flood icing means that the line details for the claws, ears and wings really stand out.

THE THANKSGIVING FEAST

The origins of Thanksgiving, held on the fourth Thursday of November, are hard to pin down, but its main purpose is not in doubt: to feast in celebration of a successful harvest. An American Thanksgiving feast has the traditional roast turkey and pumpkin pie as menu staples, but, for me, Thanksgiving provided an excuse to experiment with turkey designs. I had an idea as to how I wanted to feather the tails, inspired by the patterns on Hornsea Muramic dishes. So, these are 1970s turkeys. And fabulous, they are.

The cutters

Turkey
Pumpkin

I used two different turkey cutters for this collection. The colours and designs can be easily adapted to any shape cutter.

The biscuits

Chocolate

Icing – line

Dark brown
Blue
Made by adding the tiniest of black to a strong sky blue.
Orange
Black
White
Burgundy
Orange-yellow
Dark green
Grey
A selection of line colours for the tails
Use the colours mixed for the heads and bodies, plus some extras, if you like. I have also added avocado green.

Icing – flood

Dark brown
Blue
Orange
Black
White
Burgundy
Orange-yellow
Dark green
Grey

Blue and brown

- Outline a round section in the middle of the biscuit, using dark brown line icing, and flood with dark brown. Leave to dry. Outline the tail section with the same dark brown.

- Outline the head section with blue, and flood, leaving a section for the beak and wattle.

- For the tail, flood with dark brown icing, and add five curved stripes, using your chosen colours of line icing. Here, I used avocado green–orangey yellow–blue–brown–brown. Feather the tail, while the icing is still wet (see Decorating tip: Feather effects). Start at the outside edge of the tail and finish at the edge of the brown middle section. Leave to dry.

- Use orange–yellow line icing to fill a small beak section. Use burgundy line icing to add a small wattle, under the beak.

- With black line icing, add small lines underneath the body, for feet. Finish with a dot of black on white, for an eye.

Orange, black and brown

- Decorate as for the blue and brown turkey, but give this one an orange head, black middle and brown tail.
- For the tail feathering, I used lines of blue–white–black–orange–orange. Blue line icing was used for the beak and white line icing for the wattle.

White, black and brown

- Decorate as for the blue and brown turkey, but give this one a white head, black middle and brown tail.
- For the tail feathering, I used lines of blue–white–black–burgundy–burgundy. Orange line icing was used for the beak and burgundy line icing for the wattle.

Orange, black and white

- Note that this biscuit shape is more difficult to decorate, due to the wing detail.
- Outline the head first, using orange line icing, leaving sections for the wattle and beak, then flood.
- Outline the body and wing section, using white line icing. Do not make the section completely round, square off the tail and only outline the outside of the wing. Outline the tail section with white.
- When completely dry, flood the middle with black. While the icing is still wet, add two or three lines of line colour, to add colour to the wings. Here, I used orange–burgundy. Feather these lines upward, with four drags of a cocktail stick.
- Flood the tail section with white. While the icing is still wet, add six or seven lines of your chosen tail colours. Here, I used burgundy–black–burgundy–dark brown–orange–orange–orange. Feather the tail from the outside toward the centre.
- Add a beak with dark brown line icing, and a wattle with burgundy line icing. Add one part of the wattle and leave it to dry before adding the second, so the parts do not run together.

- Use small black lines to add the feet, and add a dot of black on white, for an eye.
- Lastly, use white line icing to go over the wing section, creating a strong white outline to show off the wing feathers.

Burgundy, brown and black

- Decorate as for the orange, black and white turkey but give this one a burgundy head, brown body and black tail. His beak is orange and the wattle blue.
- For the feather colours on the wing, I used blue-burgundy and for the tail I used blue-white-blue-burgundy-brown-brown-brown.

DECORATING TIP: **FEATHER EFFECTS**

It doesn't seem quite right that the simple cocktail stick is up there with icing nozzles and fancy food colours on the essential biscuit decorating kit list. But these humble sticks do so much. You can't do without them.

They are the tool of choice when creating feather effects in icing. Which is easy. Very easy. The finished effect looks far more intricate and professional than the effort required to create it. Here is how I used this technique to make the fabulous turkey tails.

After outlining the turkey tail, I filled it with the flood colour. Straight away, I added curved lines of colour. In this example, I used blue–white–black–orange–orange lines.

Next came the feathering. Starting at the outside edge, at the points where the tail shape indented, I gently dragged the cocktail stick inward about nine times, stopping when I reached the round, black middle section. Easy, but very effective.

Remember when feathering:

- Don't drag the cocktail stick too deeply into the icing or the icing might start to dry before the surface smooths over, leaving dents in the surface.

- Wipe the cocktail stick clean on a piece of kitchen towel after each drag. This will stop bits of icing colour ending up where you don't want them.

- Drag along the ends of the lines. You can see on the turkeys that I feathered along the line ends, at the top and bottom of the tail, so that any messy line ends were hidden and the whole tail looks neat.

- Make sure your line icing is not runny and that the icing line is quite thin. This will keep the lines sharp and distinct, and minimise colour bleed.

- Give the biscuit a shake on the table or worksurface when you have finished feathering, to smooth the surface over.

Feathering does not take very long, because you add the lines of colour to wet flood icing, and the technique can be used as part of many biscuit designs. You can see feather effects throughout this book. The Valentine's hearts on page 49 and the tropical fish on page 88 are some examples.

- In your chosen colour, ice a line around his neck for a collar. When that line is dry, add a dot of yellow for a bell. If you choose to, add gold glitter.

- For Rudolf's eye, ice on a white dot and then straight away, ice a small black dot on top.

- Lastly, give Rudolf's nose its trademark red tip.

Angel

- Outline the main body of the angel with white line icing. When dry, flood with white and leave to dry completely.

- Add sleeve detail and a dot pattern to the bottom of the angel using white line icing.

- For the angel's face, outline in skintone and fill in with the same icing. Leave a section for the hair. For the hands, ice one large blob of white, and drag upward with a cocktail stick to create a vertically positioned hand. Leave the first hand to dry before doing the second one, so the icing for the two hands does not run together.

- Add yellow lines for the hair. Similar to the Christmas tree trunks, leave gaps between the lines and add additional lines when the first ones have dried. This will create clearly defined hair.

- Ice eyelids with blue line icing, and a small round pink

mouth, to give the impression that the angel is closed eyed and singing.

- Lastly, the wings. Using yellow line icing, ice a circle at the top of the wing, in near the angel's shoulder. From here, ice four long loops to the edge of the wings, so that it is fully outlined and with a lacy effect. While the icing is still wet, add gold glitter.

Father Christmas

- He is created on a simple, circle-shaped biscuit.
- Using red line icing, create the hat by outlining a crescent section at the top. When dry, flood with red. When this is dry, add the floppy end section of the hat. With red line icing, ice a curve shape along the top of the hat, ending in a point at the left outside edge. Fill in straight away using the same icing and leave to dry.
- From the tips of the hat, at the biscuit edge, ice a similar-shaped crescent at the bottom of the biscuit in white line icing, for a beard. When dry, flood with white.
- Add a thick band of white at the bottom of the hat, to overlap slightly with the top

corners of the beard. Do this by outlining with white line icing, and then filling immediately with the same icing. Leave to dry.

- Fill in the middle section of the biscuit with skintone and leave to dry completely. Then add a white blob for a pompom on the end of the hat.
- Add the facial features. Ice two large white blobs about one-third up from the beard, then use a cocktail stick to drag the ends out to create a tapered moustache. Make sure you have applied quite a large amount of icing initially,

so there is enough to create a sizeable moustache.

- Ice two small lines near the top of the face, then tease their ends with a cocktail stick to create shaped eyebrows. Underneath add eyes: a dot of white followed by a dot of black on top. Then add two pink dots for round, rosy cheeks.
- Lastly, fill in the small gap created between moustache and beard with red line icing, for the mouth, and add an additional dot of skintone above the moustache for a nose.

Baubles

- Using your chosen colour, outline the bauble, also outlining a small circle around the hole at the top. When dry, flood with the same colour.

- **Initial bauble:** To your outlined and filled bauble, ice around the hole at the top, in your chosen line icing colour.

- Then ice two sets of parallel lines, across the top and bottom of the bauble, in line icing of your chosen colour.

- Ice a series of small dots between each pair of lines.

- Ice a letter onto the middle of the bauble. If you are not confident with lettering, practise on your kitchen worktop first.

- Ice the leaf pattern around the letter. Ice a line with a swirl at first, then add small lines to resemble leaves.

- If you want your baubles to sparkle, add glitter straight away.

- **Snowflake bauble:** To your outlined and filled bauble, outline the outside edge. Also create an outline around the top section of the bauble, and around the hole.

- Then ice a snowflake pattern in white or pale blue line icing. Ice three straight lines of even length and spacing, making sure they cross over in the middle. Then add line detail to the six line ends, to create a traditional snowflake. Then add small dots around the centre and around the edge of the bauble.

- If you want a glittery snowflake, add it while the icing is wet. I used silver, but white would also work well.

- **Daisy bauble:** To your outlined and filled bauble, outline the section at the top of the bauble, and around the hole, in your chosen line colour.

- Add a large dot to the middle, for the daisy's centre, using white line icing. Then add eight petals around the dot, by squeezing out lines of white slowly, so they are

thick enough. If you need to, use a cocktail stick to taper the ends to better resemble a petal shape. Leave to dry.

- When the bauble is completely dry, add four swirls in your chosen colour of line icing. Start at the middle and extend the swirl to the edge of the bauble. If you like, add glitter to your swirls.

- **Swirly bauble:** To your outlined and filled bauble, outline the section at the top of the bauble, and around

the hole, in your chosen line colour.

- Then create the swirl pattern. Working from the bottom left of the biscuit, ice one swirl, then another joining on to it, and then another. Keep going until you have covered the biscuit. The placement of the swirls is not so important, but do try to keep them the same size.

- Ice around the edge of the biscuit and then, if you like, add glitter.

DESIGN TIP: **BLACK OUTLINES**

Black line icing is extremely useful. I always have a bag of it stashed in the fridge and, when I am mixing some, always mix a lot because I know that, practically whatever biscuits I am decorating, there is almost always a call for black. Just flicking through the pictures of the collections in this book will show you how much it is used: every animal's eye needs a black pupil for starters.

Black can also be great for outlining. Think of how black outlines are used in iconic cartoon characters and in children's books: using black to outline biscuits in the same way can create this same striking, graphic effect.

If you wish to use black in this way, it is important to sketch out a design first. As black will be the first colour you use, and you will often be icing lines onto the body of the biscuit as well as the edge, you don't want to make mistakes. It can help to use a black food colour pen to mark out the lines, at least for the first couple of biscuits.

For the candy canes, I sketched the design so that I could make sure the red and white colour blocks

were spaced evenly on the biscuit. I then iced the black line detail and waited for it to dry. I then filled alternate sections with a thick squeeze of red flood icing, which I pushed into the corners with a cocktail stick. For some, I covered these red sections with red glitter. When the biscuits were completely dry, I brushed off the excess red glitter and then filled in the white sections.

For the snowmen on page 170, I sketched out the black parts of the design, using the body of the snowman as an edge for one part of the scarf. I then iced the black lines that marked out the scarf and hat. When the black lines were completely dry, white was then flooded around the scarf and hat outline, and I used a cocktail stick to push the white icing into the corner sections that edged the scarf. Flooding a lot of white icing right near the scarf risked the icing running over the black line. Then, when the snowman's body and face were dry, I filled in the scarf and beanie hat, using blobs of line icing pushed to the edges of the squares with cocktail sticks.

LET IT SNOW

I love the way that the symbols and images of Christmas have been extended to include all things wintry. Even my youngest daughter's Christmas stocking has a huge felt penguin on it. The association of Christmas and winter has such a cheering effect at such a cold time of year. Instead of snow being a complete nuisance, the beauty of snowflakes can be enjoyed as decorations on our trees, patterns on wrapping paper and, of course, as lovely biscuits. And, with snow, comes snowmen – the ones made of snow and, here, the ones made of gingerbread.

The cutters
A selection of snowflakes
Snowmen

The biscuits
Gingerbread
If you would like your snowflakes or snowmen to hang from a tree, put a hole in the top of the biscuit, before baking.

Icing – line
White
Black
Orange
A selection of colours of your choice, such as blue, green, red, yellow and purple.

Icing – flood
White
Black

Optional glitter
Glacier lilac
Crystal blue

Snowflakes
- Believe me when I say that, in the case of the snowflakes that are simply patterns on the gingerbread base, these are possibly the quickest and easiest biscuits to decorate in the entire book. All you need to mix up is white line icing, and to ice lines and dots to the snowflake biscuits to create patterns.

Traditional snowflake
- Outline the snowflake in white or, as I have done here, put lines on the snowflake's points. Using the biscuit's points as a guide, ice three lines from point to point, making sure the lines cross in the centre of the snowflake. Then add the detail at the six line ends, to create the feather design. Add six small dots around the centre of the snowflake.

Atomic snowflake
- Outline the snowflake in white, or add detail to the points only. Ice three long lines from point to point, crossing over in the middle. At the end of each line, and before you stop icing and lift away your icing bag, squeeze a solid ball of icing to create

the atomic ball effect. Then add three smaller lines in between the larger lines, also crossing over the centre. Finish each line with a ball of icing, as with the larger lines.

Glacier lilac, which is white, but with purple highlights, which you can see when you tilt the snowflake under light. It turns your snowflakes from sparkly white into something a little more magical.

Big snowflakes

- There are no set design rules here. In this example, I used the shape of the biscuit to guide the design, following curves and points to make a pattern. Simple line sections and sequences of dots give a beautiful finish, and you can create any number of original patterns.

- As to whether or not you add glitter to your snowflakes, that is up to you. The glitter just needs to be added while the icing is still wet. For these, very simply decorated snowflakes, I think it really adds some special sparkle. You can use plain white glitter, but my choice is

Blue on white snowflake

- Outline the entire snowflake in white. When dry, flood with white. When the snowflake is completely dry, add your snowflake design in your chosen colour. I used a pale blue here, but think other pastel colours could work as well. If you are using glitter, add it immediately, while the snowflake detail is still wet. I chose, appropriately, Crystal blue.

Snowman with top hat

- Using black line icing, outline the top hat and scarf, including square sections that can be filled later with the scarf's colours. Leave to dry before flooding the top hat with black.

- Outline the body sections of the snowman with white. When dry, flood with white and leave to dry.

- Choose your two line colours for the snowman's scarf. In alternate squares, put a decent-sized blob of your first colour. When all your blobs are in place, tease the icing into the corners of the black squares with a cocktail stick. Work quickly here, so that the icing does not start to set before you finish. Leave to dry.

- Repeat the process in the remaining scarf squares with your second colour.

- When the snowman is completely dry, add the finishing touches. For his carrot nose, add a thick line of orange, tapering the end with a cocktail stick to create a pointy end. Add black dots for his coal eyes, smile and buttons.

Snowman with beanie

- With black line icing, outline the snowman's beanie and scarf, similar to the outlines for the snowman with top hat.

- Choose your two line colours for the snowman's scarf and beanie. For the scarf and the

squares on the beanie, ice as for the snowman with top hat, placing blobs of colour in alternate squares and pushing the blobs into the corners with a cocktail stick.

- For the rest of the snowman's hat, fill in the main part with one colour, giving the biscuit a shake to smooth the finished surface. For the pompom on top, squeeze a generous ball of icing onto the top of the beanie, then use a cocktail stick to drag out small lines to create a woolly effect.

Note: I decorated both of these snowmen using black outlines. For more information on how I have done this, and on creating designs with black outlines, see the Design tip: Black outlines on page 167.

DECORATING TIP: **WHITER THAN WHITE**

You would be forgiven for thinking that, when you have mixed up a bowlful of royal icing, that it looks white. Well, you couldn't call it any other colour, but it isn't really white. To get whiter than white, that is, the white that is the white of fresh snow, you need to add white colouring.

Just a few drops of white are all that you need to transform your icing from being slightly wishy washy, almost translucent white, to toothpaste bright. Have a look at the two snowflakes in this photograph. The line icing used for both (for the

outline and the snowflake pattern) has had white colouring added. The flood icing for the snowflake on the left is uncoloured royal icing, the flood icing for the snowflake on the right has had white colour added. You may not notice a difference

at first glance but have a closer inspection. You can see the contrast between the strong, bright white snowflake on the right and the milky, greyish coloured snowflake on the left. So there you have it, a simple tip that makes a big difference when it comes to white: don't forget to colour it.

AWAY IN A MANGER

A set of nativity biscuits is not only charming, but a welcome nod to tradition. I have consciously decorated this collection using simple, natural colours to reflect Christmas' humble origins and to remind us that, just because it is Christmas, sprinkles and glitter are not always mandatory. Okay, our three wise men are a bit more colourful, but they are kings, so I have decorated them according to their status.

The cutters
Mary
Joseph
Baby in manger
Wise man
Camel
Donkey
Sheep
Star

I made this collection from a boxed set of nativity cutters. If you want to make this collection but don't have the set, the animals and star can be sourced as individual cutters, or you may have some already. The shapes for the people can then be simplified and sketched onto stiff card or plastic and cut around when placed on the dough. A bit of work, but not unmanageable.

The biscuits
Gingerbread

Icing – line
Black
White
Yellow
Pale blue
Dark blue
Ivory
Pink

Sand
Made by adding drops of yellow, orange and brown.
Skintone
Made by adding drops of pink and brown to ivory, then lightening with white.
A selection of colours for the donkey's and camel's blankets, and for the wise men. I have used blue, green, purple, yellow and red.

Icing – flood
Pale blue
Dark blue
Flood icing to match the line icing for the wise men. Here I have used blue, green, purple, yellow and red.

Decorations and optional glitter
Gold glitter
Coloured balls (dragees) and jelly sweets

Mary

- Outline Mary's robe in pale blue, and flood with the same colour blue. Leave sections of biscuit for her sandal, face and head covering. When dry, ice on top of the robe with the blue line icing, adding fold and sleeve detail.

- For her sandals, add a cross pattern over her foot in brown.

- Outline her head covering in ivory, and then fill with the same icing. Outline and fill her face with skintone, in the same way.

- When dry, add hands by adding two skintone dots at the top of her sleeves.

Adding a first dot and then letting it dry before adding the second will stop the dots running together. When dry, add a smaller dot above the larger dots, for thumbs.

- Lastly, add her facial features. I gave her blue eyes – a pale blue dot with smaller black dot for a pupil. Then ice a pink line for a smile and two pink dots for rosy cheeks.

Joseph

- Outline the section for Joseph's robe with dark blue line icing, leaving sections for his sandals, face and headcloth. Flood with dark blue. When dry, add dark blue line icing to mark out a sleeve.
- Add Joseph's sandal in the same way as Mary's – a cross

pattern over the foot in brown line icing.

- For his headcloth, use sand-coloured line icing to outline the shape, and then fill in with the same icing. When dry, outline and fill the section for his face, using skintone.
- For Joseph's beard and moustache, ice lines of brown. Ice a couple of lines and leave to dry before adding a couple more lines, so that the dried lines resemble hair. Ice downward lines to represent his moustache when the beard has dried.
- Add eyes by icing on two small white dots, followed by two smaller black dots. Tiny lines of black can then be added to represent eyebrows. Add a dot of skintone for a nose.
- Lastly, add some detail to Joseph's clothes. A line of brown around his headcloth and two lines of brown on the edge of his sleeve.

Baby in the manger

- Outline the bottom part of the biscuit in brown line icing, to represent the wooden manger. Flood with brown. When dry, outline and

fill a section for the swaddled baby on top of the brown, using pale blue line icing. Leave a section for the baby's face.

- When completely dry, add yellow hay. Add yellow lines in one direction, then leave to dry. Add more yellow lines, and leave to dry. Keep adding more lines, leaving a few minutes in between each lot. Keep going until you have enough yellow lines to show a good amount of hay for the baby to rest in, and the point where the brown and blue icing meet is sufficiently covered.

- Outline and fill the baby's tiny face, in skintone. When dry, add a tiny pink dot for a mouth, and a tiny blue curved line for his eyelid, so he looks asleep.

Wise men

- I decorated all three wise men the same way. The only variation is the colours chosen. Here, I describe how I decorated Caspar, wearing blue and carrying gold. I should add that there are many ways you can decorate a wise man – I simply adapted a design from a Christmas card.

- For his large sleeve, outline a roughly rectangular shape in dark blue, leaving a small section for his hand and gift. Flood with dark blue when dry. When dry, add another sleeve outline in dark blue, to mark it out clearly against the rest of the robe.

- Outline the front section of his robe in the same dark blue, and flood when dry.

- For his head covering, outline a rectangular band of dark blue using line icing and fill using the same icing. While wet, outline the three sections at the top, to fill later. Leave to dry.

- For his cape, outline in purple and then flood when dry.

- For his face, outline and fill a roughly triangular shape, using skintone. Do not fill in the section all the way down to the top of the sleeve, leave a section for his beard. Fill in the small section at the end of his sleeve for his hand. Leave to dry completely.

- For the diamond pattern on his cape and robe, I iced an arrangement of dots. The points for the diamonds were then teased out from the dot using a cocktail stick. You need to work quickly here, so that your dots don't dry before you turn them into diamonds, or only do one or two at a time.

- For his beard, fill in the small section between his face and sleeve with brown line icing. Add another small triangle to fill in the small corner near the corner of his sleeve and the edge of his hat. When dry, add a downward line for a moustache.

- I chose brown eyes for my wise men – a dot of brown followed by a smaller dot of black.

- Lastly, add the sections that are to be glittered, if you so choose, using yellow line icing. Fill in the top sections of the head covering, add yellow lines down the robe and on the sleeve, and a large yellow ball in his hand, to represent his gift of gold. Apply the gold glitter straight away.

- To create the boxes of frankincense and myrrh, the gifts of Melchior and Balthasar, I used silver dragees and jelly sweets. Melchoir has a section of sweet cut into a small square and decorated with two lines of green icing. A silver dragee is stuck onto the top of the box with red icing. The box was then stuck onto his hand with skintone icing.

- Balthasar has a triangular box, again made from a jelly sweet, and decorated with a v-shaped line of yellow, which has had gold glitter added. A silver dragee was stuck to the top and the box stuck to his hand in the same way as Melchoir's box.

muzzle and ears. Do not outline a section on his back, where his saddlecloth is to go.

- When dry, outline and fill a saddlecloth, in a colour of your choice. Add dots and tassels in contrasting colours, being sure to let each application of icing dry before adding another, to keep the dots defined and to avoid colour bleed.

- For his hooves, ice one dot of brown on each foot. Allow to dry before adding the second dot.

- Finish with an eye – a small dot of black on white.

Camel

- Using sand-coloured line icing, outline the camel's body, leaving a gap on his hump for a blanket.

- For his hairy neck and knees, add small, rough lines of sand icing. Leave some gaps between the lines and then

add more lines when the first lot has dried, so the icing does not run together.

- Using the same sand icing, add line detail for the camel's ear and fill in his nose.

- Create a blanket in the same way as for the donkey, but use different colours. Only add new colours and patterns when icing that has already been applied has dried.

- For his hooves, add dots, similar to the donkey. Allow the first dot to dry on each foot before adding the second, or leave a small gap between the two dots, so they do not run together.

- Finish the camel with an eye – small black dot on white, and a line of upturned black for a mouth.

Sheep

- Using white line icing, ice small, squiggly swirls onto

Donkey

- Outline the donkey shape in brown, adding extra line details to define his legs, tail,

the body of the sheep, to create wool. Leave the icing to dry a little bit between adding sets of squiggles, or simply don't add too many. Don't add so much that the lines run together or the circular, woolly pattern is lost.

- Add black dots for his feet, nose and tail. Finish by adding a dot of black on a dot of white for an eye, and a

tiny dot of white detail at the tip of the sheep's nose.

Star
- Outline around the edge of the star with yellow line icing. Using the same icing, outline a second star inside the first, and fill in using the same icing. If you like, add gold glitter while the icing is still wet.

DECORATING TIP: USING LINE ICING TO FILL

Making royal icing, colouring it, and getting the right consistencies for line icing and flood icing can be very time-consuming, particularly if you are decorating a collection that calls for decorating lots of small sections of biscuit with lots of different colours.

For this reason, a quick shortcut that works is to fill in small biscuit sections with line icing, rather than flood icing. I used this technique a lot when decorating this collection, as there were so many small sections – faces, hands, beards, saddlecloths and so on. In fact, anywhere I have stated 'outline and fill', or similar, instead of outline and flood.

Using this technique works because only small amounts of icing are used, thereby removing the need for the defined, dried dam wall of outline icing that is used when flooding larger areas. It also removes the

outline that is often left behind on a biscuit when the icing has dried. Have a look at this close up of the baby in the manger. You can see where I outlined the wooden manger and allowed it to dry before flooding it. For the baby's swaddling and his wee face, however, I outlined and filled using line icing only, and while the outline was still wet, creating a uniform finish.

This trick can save a lot of time when mixing colours and when decorating. The one potential pitfall is dents and divots in your dried icing, because line icing is thicker than flood, so does not smooth over as easily. To avoid this, use line icing to fill small sections only, apply quite a lot of icing to get effective coverage, and give the biscuit a good shake on top of the table or workbench as soon as you have applied the icing. This will make sure the icing dries with a flat surface.

BRILLIANT BISCUITS
FOR CHILDREN

BAKING AND DECORATING WITH CHILDREN

If you have children, you can't keep them away from your biscuit hobby for long.

Presumably, they will have been eating your creations anyway so they will be wise as to what you are up to. How much you let them get involved will depend on their age and your levels of patience but it can be fun for both of you.

Don't expect perfect lines and dots, or your kitchen to stay clean, but be prepared to be charmed by their efforts. Every time I do biscuit decorating with children I am wowed: while I can spend hours perfecting a design, a child's imagination can – in minutes – produce a messy, colour-clashing, over-iced biscuit that is simply enchanting.

Before you let your children loose with an icing bag, here are my tips for making the biscuiting experience fun, rather than fraught.

- Mum is the boss. Always.
- Wash hands, wear apron, tie hair back.
- Get out everything you need before you start, be it for baking or decorating.

- If you want to get children to help with the baking, have the dough made first. For a child, this is the least interesting part of the whole process. Rolling dough and cutting shapes can be fun, having mum bark at you to keep away from the food mixer while it is creaming butter and sugar isn't.
- Give each child 'their' portion of dough, to roll and cut the shapes they want. Otherwise you will undoubtedly get annoyed when, after you have rolled out a whole big section of dough, they inevitably slam down a cutter smack in the middle of it.
- Remember the rule regarding the oven. That is, don't let them near it. After a tray of freshly baked biscuits comes out, lift the baking parchment off the tray and transfer it to a board. This will speed the cooling process, so your child will then be able to handle the biscuits sooner.

- When making the icing, give your child the job of choosing some icing colours, with the proviso that the lids stay on. My daughter loves lining up the little bottles and picking out her favourites.
- Don't let them squeeze out the colours from the bottles. This can only result in food colouring going everywhere. Instead, give them the job of stirring the colour in. Children love watching the bright colour swirl through the white icing.
- If your children are young, say under five, don't give them icing bags to use. They won't be able to manipulate them. Stick with flood icing in bottles. They will be able to squeeze icing out of them easily enough, and they won't particularly care how thickly it comes out, or even where it ends up.
- For older children, you can teach them how to hold and use an icing bag. Their lines will be all wobbly, but they will be able to do simple patterns and dots easily enough.
- Sprinkles are fun, but don't supply too many. With younger children particularly, there is a tendency to pile them on, to the point that the biscuit becomes three-dimensional.
- Don't get mad at children for licking their fingers. They can't help themselves, it is a deep compulsion. I have, more than once, found my daughter scratching off dried spots of icing from my kitchen work surface to eat.
- Praise their efforts, no matter how random their design or messy the execution. As much as biscuit decorating is a creative process for adults, it is for children as well. I have run decorating classes with many, many children and there has not been one that has not been proud of what they have created.

THE BIRTHDAY BISCUIT DECORATING PARTY

Predictably, I have had biscuit decorating as an activity practically every year for my daughter's birthday party. I am not sure whether, if I omitted it one year, the guests would be aghast, or relieved.

But every year, it has been a hit. It is simple to set up, easy for them to do, suits boys and girls and, the best bit, can keep them occupied for ages.

Here is how to go about it.

- Decide upon a simple party theme that the children can identify with. For my daughter's first biscuit decorating party, she was turning three and the theme was simply 'animals'. Ducks, frogs and so on. Other suitable biscuits are ones that are very open as to how they are decorated, such as hearts and stars. Having said that, children almost never interpret biscuits literally. I have seen a bright blue labrador.
- Bake the biscuits well in advance. Because biscuits keep for so long, you can keep all the last-minute party preparation to, well, the last minute.

- Make the icing a day or two before as well. If you have icing bottles, use them. You really need to have about one per person so that, at any one point, no child will be stuck without a bottle. If you don't have enough, use whatever icing bottles you have, and supplement them with icing-filled plastic bowls and paintbrushes. Cover the tops with cling film and store in a cool place overnight if you don't have room in your fridge, and give the icing a good stir before the children start decorating.
- When mixing up your colours, double up on colours that you know will be popular. For young girls, you really need two bottles or bowls of pink, for example. I find it easier to stick to fewer colours and have multiple bottles of them, rather than trying to get in every colour in the rainbow.
- Have a selection of sweets, but avoid the really small sprinkles, such as dragees. It will just be too messy. Go for bigger stuff. Dolly

mix, mini marshmallows, jelly beans, Smarties and small sugar-coated jellies are perfect. I tip the contents of the packets out onto trays or into containers for the children to help themselves.

- Plate up the biscuits beforehand, and use paper plates. This way, everyone can get given a plate with the same number of biscuits on each.

- As for how many biscuits to allocate each child, it really depends on their age. Older children, and I am talking those older than about seven or eight, have longer staying power and can become absorbed in what they are doing, so you can give them more. The big plus here is that you probably don't need to organise anything else, activity-wise. A plate of six biscuits could easily keep them going for about 45 minutes. Younger children, such as three- or four-year-olds, flag quicker, and each 'masterpiece' can be created very quickly. Limit the biscuits to three or four each.

- While the children are busy decorating, go around with a pen and write their name or initial on the edge of the plate. Each child should recognise their plate when it is time to go home, but you will speed the pick-ups and exits if you know exactly whose biscuits are whose.

- Expect some biscuits (and a lot of the sweets), to be eaten during the activity, particularly if the children are younger in age. If you want the biscuits to be taken home, whisk the plate away from the child as soon as they are finished.

- Biscuit decorating means you can, if you are organised enough, dispense with the trinket-filled party bag. As soon as each child has finished decorating, shove the plate into an

oven set at 70° Celsius/160° Fahrenheit with the fan on. They will be dry in about 15 or 20 minutes (though if the icing has been laid on really thick, they might take longer). When they are dry, pop the biscuits into a suitable bag for the child to take home. If you want to go with the biscuit party bag option, it makes sense to do the decorating activity earlier on at the party. Even if the guests end up taking home the biscuits still on the plate, this is fine. They have a take-home that contains sugar. You are covered.

THE CHRISTMAS BISCUIT DECORATING PARTY

As an activity for children, I don't limit biscuit decorating to birthday parties. It is a wonderful thing to do at Christmas.

After all, so much of Christmas is about family traditions. Each child's particular stocking or advent calendar, the exact combination of things left out for Father Christmas, and so on. Christmas baking is part of these traditions. In our family, that means biscuits, among other festive treats.

If you would like to hold a Christmas biscuit decorating party for children, read through the tips I provide on the previous pages for biscuit decorating birthday parties,

as they also apply here. Even if a full-on party isn't your thing, an afternoon decorating biscuits with your own children at a time of year when it isn't so easy to get out to the park anyway can be immensely satisfying.

Here are some additional, Christmas-specific, tips.

- The biscuits have to be gingerbread. What else?
- If you are planning on hanging the biscuits on

a tree, put holes in the tops of the biscuits before baking them. I have a tiny circle cutter just for this, but a strong drinking straw also works. Alternatively, make a hole with the end of a skewer. Just make sure the hole is big enough to thread cord or string through. And don't make the hole right near the edge of the biscuit.

- Go for your festive shapes, obviously, but the most effective ones are those that are either simple, or can be loaded with bright colours. Baubles, candy canes, trees and snowflakes are my favourites. Children always seem to go for snowmen for some reason, and little girls just love decorating angel biscuits. I wouldn't recommend including Father Christmas in the mix, simply because he is hard to decorate.

- When mixing up your icing colours, go for the obligatory red and green, but make up more than one bottle or bowl of white. Snowflakes, snowmen, angels: they all need white. But don't limit your colours to the traditional Christmas palette. Little girls will still want their pink.

- Stock up on the Christmas-themed sprinkles. Silver balls are perfect here, and you can easily supplement these with others that the supermarkets stock in abundance at this time of year.

- If you are hanging the decorations on the tree, bear in mind that they will soften up, as they are not being 'stored' in an airtight container. If the biscuits are likely to be eaten within a few days, this doesn't matter. If you want them to last longer, put the biscuits in cellophane bags, tie the bags with ribbon, then loop the ribbon on the tree branch.

- Don't underestimate the gift potential of biscuits decorated by children. They may not be perfectly executed, but they will have a certain home-made charm. Aunts, grandmothers and godparents will love them. If you have young visitors to your home over the Christmas period, let them choose a biscuit from the tree as a gift – it may even make it home to their own tree. Or not.

HELP! MY BISCUIT HAS....

...the icing colours bleeding together

Colour bleed is apparent if you can see one icing colour leeching into the colour next to it. Have a look at this turkey. You can see the black colour bleeding into the white. This is a frustrating problem, especially as it will only become apparent once the icing has dried, and by then there is nothing you can do about it. Here are some preventative measures.

- **Avoid icing strongly contrasting colours next to each other.** This is not to say you should never, ever, decorate with black icing next to white, but if you are worried about colour bleed and other colour options are available, go for colours that are similar in tone and depth of colour.
- **Make sure you have used meringue powder in your royal icing.** I am unsure why, but meringue powder seems to make a more stable royal icing, that is less prone to colour bleed.
- **Use white colouring.** If you are decorating with white, colour it white. If you are decorating with colours that you know will be placed next to strong, contrasting colours, try to use white colour when mixing. For example, a pale pink created with just a small dot of pink colour seems to be more bleed-resistant

if the colour is mixed by adding a bit more pink colour and then lightening it with white. It just seems to work.
- **Dry your biscuits quickly.** I find that colour bleed is more of a problem if newly iced biscuits are left to dry slowly, particularly in humid conditions. Get them in the oven, with the fan on, and dried quickly.

...blotchy patches in the icing

It can be extremely disheartening if, after you have taken the time to bake and decorate a batch of biscuits, you get up the next morning, have a peek, and find that your icing has gone all blotchy as it has dried. This wombat biscuit has a clear case of the blotches, which were certainly not intentional. While I have only had this problem happen very occasionally, if it happens to you, there are ways to avoid it happening again.

- **Decorate in dry conditions.** Royal icing dries best in dry conditions. Warm, humid conditions can cause the fats in your biscuit to seep up into the icing, causing blotches. To remove this risk, get your icing dry quickly. Put them, after each icing colour has been applied, back into your oven with the fan on. I have heard of other people putting their biscuits in front of a fan, but haven't tried this.

I have also read about people putting dehumidifiers in the room they are working in, or making sure the air conditioning (if they have it) is on.

- **Don't make your royal icing too thin or watery.** The problem here is that a high liquid content (egg white and water) in your royal icing means it will separate quickly. You may not notice this so much when the icing is wet, but, once dried, you could end up with blotches. Error on the side of making your icing thick, rather than thin. And make sure it is very well mixed before using, so the liquid content is thoroughly amalgamated with the icing sugar.

- **Bake crisp, dry biscuits.** If you have experienced blotching, and are decorating during the warmer summer months, bake your biscuits for a minute or so longer. This will produce a drier biscuit, less likely to leech fats into the icing.

- **Use freshly made icing.** Recycling your royal icing is tempting, though you will get a better finish on your biscuits the fresher your icing is. Icing that has spent some time in the fridge will start to separate, risking a blotchy finish when it dries. Time to confess: the wombat was made using brown icing that had been lurking around for a while. I recommend not keeping your icing for more than a few days and, even if is only one day old, mixing it again thoroughly before using it.

...air bubbles in the icing

For me, this is the most common and frustrating problem that can turn up when decorating biscuits. Especially as, experience has told me, that air bubbles can appear in two ways. The first type of air bubble occurs when air is trapped in

your flood icing and struggles to rise to the surface. What you can get are tiny raised dots on the surface of your biscuit that look, and I can't think of a better comparison, like tiny pimples. You can see this effect on this baby's kerchief, if you look closely. There are a few tiny raised spots, which are air bubbles in the icing trying to escape. The second type occurs most often where there are thick, small sections of line or flood icing. Raised spots, even thick lines are prone. What happens is that, as the icing surface dries first, the icing underneath is still wet and the surface collapses, creating small craters in your finished icing. You can see the problem with this house's rooftop. I used quite thick line icing and, as I moved the icing bag around the top of the roof, I naturally slowed down, creating a very thick spot of icing. This collapsed as it dried, producing the little craters. What to do?

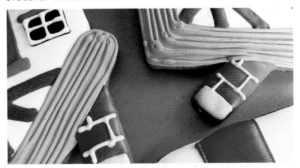

- **Don't use a whisk to mix your icing.** A whisk whips more air into your icing. If you have a freestanding food mixer, using the flat paddle attachment is fine.

- **Pour from a height.** When decanting your mixed icing into food bottles, do so from a height and pour in a thin stream. As you do, you will see the air bubbles breaking in the icing stream as it flows into the bottle. This will get rid of some of them.

- **Give your icing time to settle before using.** After you have filled up your icing bottles, let them rest for a couple of hours before using, if you have time. Then, whack the bottom of the bottle on your work surface. This will help any air bubbles near the surface break and be gone.

- **Pop air bubbles with a cocktail stick.** After flooding a biscuit, give it a few shakes back and forth across your table or work surface. Scan over the surface and look for air bubbles. Pop any that you see with a cocktail stick. Decorating under a decent lamp will show up the bubbles more easily.

- **Avoid thick line icing.** Thinner lines are far less prone to the crater effect that I have described. If you are filling small sections of a biscuit with line icing, don't apply it too thickly. You will avoid the craters if you apply a smaller amount, and then spread it out with a cocktail stick.

- **Spread out your spots.** If you are adding large, blobby spots to a biscuit, such as those on some of my Valentine's hearts, circle through the wet icing with a cocktail stick to spread and flatten the spots a little. This will help stop the thick icing collapsing and craters appearing.

- **Use quick fixes.** If your dried icing shows little craters or holes from air bubbles, simply fill them in with more icing, smooth them over (a soft paintbrush works here) and leave to dry.

...broken

This scarcely needs explaining. Biscuits break. The obvious solution is to eat the broken bits, but if you need to carry out a salvage operation, it can be done.

- **Glue the broken bits back together.** Simply splodge some line icing onto the broken edges and push the biscuit pieces back together. The royal icing will act like glue, sticking the pieces together as it dries. However, this quick fix only really works if you are then planning to flood the repaired biscuit. The flood layer will hide the join and also provide another layer of icing to strengthen the repair. It does work – have a look at the grey British fighter plane biscuit on page 133. Here is the underside of the actual biscuit, showing where I glued on a very broken wing.

After all I have said here, remember that what you are creating is still a biscuit that will, inevitably, be eaten. Those doing the eating are unlikely to notice any imperfections. They will simply be grateful that you have given them something so nice. I also think perfection is a step too far. You don't want to produce something that looks like it is machine-produced in a factory. A few wobbly lines or blemishes are fine, because your biscuit is not some industrial product but has been hand-made, by you, at home.

SUPPLIERS

All of the following companies have helped fill my kitchen cupboards with biscuit decorating equipment and supplies.

In addition, many readers will, if they are lucky enough, live close to a local cake decorating or baking supplies shop. I have a couple in my area and actively support them. I believe it is worth building a relationship with a good local business – not only do they rely on their local customers, but they will often order things in for you and are fantastic sources of advice.

Cakes, Cookies and Crafts
www.cakescookiesandcraftsshop.co.uk
01524 389684
An extensive selection of cutters, nozzles, cellophane bags, food colours, edible glitter and plenty of other speciality baking and decorating supplies.

Ebay
www.ebay.co.uk
It might seem obvious, but there are many ebay traders operating baking and decorating supplies shops, and you can often find one-off biscuit cutters for sale. This is also where I source my wooden coffee stirrers.

Kuhn Rikon
www.kuhnrikon.co.uk
01902 458410
Great decorating sets that include icing bottles and nozzles.

Lakeland
www.lakeland.co.uk
01539 488100
A great baking, decorating and cookware all-rounder. Cutters, icing bottles, nozzles, cellophane bags and plenty of other general bakeware.

Squires Kitchen
www.squires-shop.com
0845 61 71 810
Food colours, cutters and much more. A very extensive range of baking and decorating supplies.

The Cake Decorating Company
www.thecakedecoratingcompany.co.uk
0115 822 4521
A wide range of food colours, as well as meringue powder.

TK Maxx
www.tkmaxx.com
01923 473561
For cutters, icing sets and bakeware.

Two Chicks
www.twochicks.co.uk
0207 629 0972
Liquid egg whites, in cartons, all ready to be mixed into icing sugar.

US suppliers
Currently, US companies have far, far greater supplies of biscuit decorating equipment, particularly cutters. I have used all of the following, and recommend their excellent service as well as their range of products. All will ship to the UK.

American Tradition Cookie Cutters
www.americantraditioncookiecutters.com
More cutters than you could ever think of.

Copper Gifts
www.coppergifts.com
Wonderful copper cutters and a great range of food colours, all in one place.

Ecrandal
www.ecrandal.com
Beautiful, unique, handmade copper cutters.

Sugarcraft
www.sugarcraft.com
A huge range of cutters and food colours.

Ultimate Baker
www.ultimatebaker.com
A massive range of cutters as well as food colours and meringue powder.

INDEX